MICROFINANCE:
AN ECONOMIC ANALYSIS OF
BANKING
—— TO THE POOR ——

SAMUEL WAHLEN

ARCHWAY
PUBLISHING

Archway Publishing books may be ordered through booksellers or by contacting:

Archway Publishing
1663 Liberty Drive
Bloomington, IN 47403
www.archwaypublishing.com
1 (888) 242-5904

ISBN: 978-1-4808-4709-5 (sc)
ISBN: 978-1-4808-4710-1 (e)

Library of Congress Control Number: 2017942870

Print information available on the last page.

Archway Publishing rev. date: 06/26/2017

CONTENTS

INTRODUCTION

We live in an amazing time. The pace at which technology is improving is absolutely remarkable. Between the headlines of the latest celebrity relationship breakups and major court cases, one can see news of the latest innovations—accomplishments that have the potential to revolutionize our way of life. As some individuals get new smart phones and others benefit from the great strides being made in medical fields, it seems that civilization is rapidly progressing. However, amid this progress, some are being left behind. Many do not enjoy the impact of all this change as the blessings of the technological innovation transforming our culture. For hundreds of millions of people around the world, challenging times do not show any signs of becoming easier. As if struggling with the weight of the world on their shoulders, many bear the burden of poverty.

Poverty destroys everything that is optimistic and positive about life. It forces people to live in horrible conditions, work miserable hours for nearly nonexistent pay, and become vulnerable to devastating environmental destruction and deadly diseases. It is no mystery that the places where people suffer the most from famine, illness, and violence are countries that remain largely underdeveloped and have some of the highest rates of poverty. The poor find themselves trapped. They struggle to feed their families. They work long hours for little pay. They need every bit of their earnings to put food on the table and roofs over their heads. They feel trapped. Unable to save, make improvements to their living conditions, or educate themselves or their children, they see no end to the nightmare. They suffer health issues due to poorly structured homes, bad habits and diet, and challenging lifestyles. Infection spreads quickly and is hard to prevent. These health issues force many of the poorest of the poor to make additional sacrifices to pay for health care, compounding an already difficult situation.

As the poor struggle, criminals and terrorist groups take advantage of the situation. Throughout history, extremist groups have used poverty to justify violence. They persuade their neighbors and families that other people are to blame for their situation. In some developing countries, such as Afghanistan or Columbia, people resort to growing illegal drugs, which eventually make their way to the United States. Furthermore, criminals might convince poor youth that crime is their only possible escape from a dim future. Often, the poor become pawns, used and preyed upon by evil people. Dictators use persuasive rhetoric to get the support of depressed and disenchanted populaces. Like bullies in a schoolyard, local crime bosses or corrupt and power hungry politicians rob, cheat, and abuse the poor.

It is a shame that poverty still exists to such an extent. Human beings should not have to live in such dire circumstances. While some make bad decisions that lead to poverty, many never even have a choice. Born into poverty, they find it impossible to escape.

When helping the poor, the goal does not need to be unanimous economic equality. Instead, the focus should be to provide opportunity to those that seek to escape the clutches of poverty.

Unfortunately, when discussing poverty, it's easy to lose an audience. People can become lethargic and disinterested, sensing hopelessness and feeling apathy. People are quick to ask what the point is or why they should help those on the other side of the world when there are people struggling nearby. Both are very fair questions and deserve answers. People often use theological texts to reinforce their responses. However, there are more than moral and ethical reasons to help those in need. For starters, assisting the poor can offer both economic and security benefits.

Economically speaking, poverty is harmful to everyone. Economic development breeds economic development. Businesses do better when more people can afford their products. When businesses do better, they spend money to make improvements, construct new buildings and expand operations, and hire additional employees. Therefore, everyone has an incentive for others to be wealthier. A business owner needs people to buy the company's products or services. A construction worker needs businesses to grow and people to buy new homes or make home improvements. The more people can afford goods and services, the more potential customers there are.

The same is true internationally. When individuals and businesses are financially stronger in country A, they can and will purchase more products and equipment from country B. However, the opposite is also true. If county A is poor, then it will buy fewer products and services from country B. In real world terms, if South Africa experiences high levels of economic growth and the median income levels rise, its citizens will be able to afford more American products. However, if South Africa goes through a recession and has negative economic growth, it will decrease its imports from countries like the United States.

In addition, the United States has a national security motive for combating poverty in foreign countries. Although it would be easy and convenient to assume that the United States does not need and is not impacted by small, underdeveloped countries, this is a false and dangerous supposition. As seen by the horrible events on September 11, 2001, the United States is not immune to the activities of groups in other countries. Terrorist and criminal organizations use poverty to legitimize their groups and recruit new members. Eliminating poverty or creating alternative opportunities undermines their operations. There may always be criminals and violent individuals, but creating economic development can handicap their recruiting and reduce profits as the poor see alternatives to growing illegal drugs. Bullies are only powerful when no one opposes them. Helping poor individuals create income-generating activities allows them to have a voice in their communities. Just as the middle class has strengthened democratic institutions in the United States, it can do so in other countries.

If the United States desires to expand trade, create jobs, and strengthen its national security, we must address the fundamental issues behind the problems we face. The poor must be engaged in the international economy and become trading partners. They need ways of producing income if we hope to eliminate the terrorist organizations that plague their communities. The poor have to be able to afford our products if we wish to have them purchase them.

We can accomplish this without government assistance or donating billions of dollars. There is an alternative approach to combating poverty that allows for mutually beneficial outcomes— microfinance. The poor are given a hand up instead of a handout. Instead of throwing money at the problem, businesses and nonprofits can lend money to the poor and provide financial services in a manner that the poorest of the poor can afford and benefit from. This book will explain the concept of microfinance, discuss its relevance, and analyze its potential.

Microfinance, the field of financial services directed toward the poor in developing countries, has been growing since its creation in the 1970s. Although its success has been difficult to properly estimate, microfinance could very well be the alternative approach that the poor need. The current state of foreign and economic development efforts is disappointing. Trillions of dollars have been thrown into the abyss in unsuccessful attempts to eliminate poverty. Furthermore, some economists have claimed that the aid is actually hurting the poor. The introduction of microfinance and its wide range of services may be a solution. Through the creation and expansion of small businesses in developing countries, we can create economic growth and help families climb out of the poverty trap. However, before throwing all of our energy and capital behind microfinance, it is important to determine if it is a worthwhile investment. The purpose of microfinance is to empower the poor through an affordable, if not profitable, method.

The poor deserve the time and attention it takes to create a solution. Furthermore, we have incentives to invest in fighting poverty. In a time of innovation and possibility, we can make a world where everyone is a trading partner and can enjoy the many benefits of capitalism and free markets. We can create that world—a world of opportunity.

CHAPTER 1

FOREIGN AID IS A FAILURE

E very year, governments and well-meaning nonprofits spend fortunes and dedicate countless hours attempting to eradicate poverty and heal its symptoms. Despite the billions of dollars flowing into developing countries throughout the world, there is little to show for these efforts. While the intentions of donors and governments are generous and admirable, there appears to be little correlation between economic growth and foreign aid. Furthermore, there appears to be evidence that aid makes the plight of the poor worse and weakens democratic institutions in developing countries. One Kenyan economist, James Shikwati (2005), argued that: "If the industrial nations really want to help the Africans, they should finally terminate this awful aid. The countries that have collected the most development aid are also the ones that are in the worst shape. Despite the billions that have poured in to Africa, the continent remains poor." In fact, very few studies show that aid has a substantial positive impact.

As Shikwati says, Africa is commonly used as an example of how foreign aid goes wrong. The African continent has received more aid than any other area in the world, yet there is little tangible evidence of its success. While some improvements have been made with technology, international trade, and aid from outside agencies and NGOs, much of Africa continues to be full of uncertainty and instability with high rates of disease and infant mortality and millions of extremely poor families.

Unfortunately, much of the foreign aid given to developing countries has made matters worse. Shikwati (2005) goes on to say that aid has caused many problems for Africa's people and limited their ability to combat poverty:

> Huge bureaucracies are financed (with the aid money), corruption and complacency are promoted, Africans are taught to be beggars and not to be independent. In addition, development aid weakens the local markets everywhere and dampens the spirit of entrepreneurship that we so desperately need. As absurd as it may sound: Development aid is one of the reasons for Africa's problems. If the West were to cancel these payments, normal Africans wouldn't even notice. Only the functionaries would be hard hit. Which is why they maintain that the world would stop turning without this development aid [sic].

Although they have the best of intentions, NGOs and governmental agencies are harming those that they intend to help. By providing food and clothing to the poor in developing countries, they cause local farmers and textile companies to struggle to survive or even enter the market because they are unable to compete with the low prices. Entrepreneurs cannot sell the same items that NGOs are giving away for free. Furthermore, the incentive to start and grow a business is reduced because NGOs and governmental agencies often create conditions that discourage entrepreneurs. The offer of free food, shelter, education, and clothing, destroys the need to risk starting a business. Much of the aid given to the poor stipulates that individuals receiving it not have a successful business or wealth of any kind. With these types of rules in place, why would anyone jeopardize their family's access to food and supplies by starting a business that could fail?

To try to help local markets, NGOs and government development agencies often purchase food and supplies from local businesses. However, in doing so, they can destroy the area's local markets. The outside organizations select winners and losers by buying from some and not from others. Those that are lucky enough to sell to NGOs are able to lower their prices in other areas, invest their profits in ways that lower costs, and take other measures that help them corner the market. Meanwhile, those businesses that are not able to sell to the development organizations can no longer compete. Furthermore, they lose customers that qualify for the aid and therefore no longer need to buy from them.

While the intentions of those who provide foreign aid are often positive, foreign aid has often weakened democratic institutions in developing countries. Shikwati says that corrupt governments can stay in power because they are financed by foreign aid or because private aid reduces the impact of their nefarious actions. Lael Brainard (2003, 152), at the Brookings Institute, notes, "The history of US assistance is littered with tales of corrupt foreign officials using aid to line their own pockets, support military buildups, and pursue vanity projects. It is no wonder that few studies show clear correlations between aid flows and growth." Governmental aid often gets misdirected, resulting in funding hostile governments that are cruel to their people. Aid ends up becoming a tool for political means and purposes; the goal of assisting the poor and endangered is lost. When nations and donors decide which nations will receive aid and how much, the poor can easily become an afterthought. Decisions are made based upon political connections and lobbying, which nations have strong national security interests and might consider which countries could bring favorable news attention. In addition to these motivations, nations use foreign aid as a tool to build relationships with other nations or as leverage in negotiations. These criteria often mean that the poor are the losers, rarely to benefit from the money spent in their name. The leaders who receive this funding often use it to finance their personal ambitions directly or indirectly, by cutting funding that would have been spent on social programs that are now covered by foreign aid. Additionally, aid can be used to cover up fraud or poor policy-making. When disaster strikes or war erupts, instead of holding leaders accountable for their actions, the people see the leaders bragging about bringing in aid and creating social programs with other countries' money. Those social programs and aid are only temporary solutions to the problem of failed governments.

NGOs and governmental agencies often boast about the positive work they are doing without understanding the unintentional effects. Even if one assumes that the work they are doing is positive and has a great impact, the negative consequences far outweigh any possible benefit. By spending millions helping the poor in developing countries, donors are empowering leaders to continue making bad policy decisions. The programs are expensive, have no long-term success in ending poverty, and often reinforce the corrupt and failed governments that cause the problems. If this issue is to ever be resolved, development theorist and policymakers need to reevaluate foreign aid.

Foreign aid, although a nice idea, fails to address the fundamental problems facing developing countries. While there are often a multitude of challenges to overcoming poverty, the key component is empowering and enabling countries to fix their own problems. Issues such as poverty and inequality must be addressed within. Outside aid can be helpful, especially in times of disaster, but should not be the major motivator of development. Often, outside organizations and groups enter impoverished countries and dedicate large amount of supplies and finances to temporary solutions, but fail to establish long-term revenue-producing activities for the poor. Therefore, when the funding from the outside groups dries up or is redirected, the poor are left behind and forgotten. Resources are finite; without addressing the fundamental cause of poverty, limited resources will continue flowing into a seemingly endless abyss. Poverty can never be fully eradicated unless the poor can climb the economic ladder and grow their incomes on their own. Thanks to a gentleman named Mohammad Yunus, there appears to be a way to accomplish this goal.

CHAPTER 2

SMALL BUSINESSES CAN COMBAT POVERTY

While the majority of development efforts go toward improving the quality of life for the very poor or connecting them with salaried employment, some attention has gone to studying small businesses and the positive impact that they have on the poor. Since the 1950s, small enterprise has played a role, albeit a minimal one, in development thinking, but only due to the prospect that small businesses might become grander. They have rarely been viewed as a solution in and of themselves (Alila 2001). The consensus has been that small or micro sized businesses could only be helpful in addressing poverty if they grew into large corporations and hired the more of the poor. There did not appear to be any thought that micro enterprises could be the predominant factor in pulling people out of extreme poverty.

Part of this position rests on the assumption that the poor cannot help themselves. Often in development theory, economists and policymakers overlook the skills and abilities that poor individuals may have. Instead, it is assumed that they need someone to train them, help them become civilized, and give them employment; it is generally not considered that poor individuals could create and operate their own businesses.

This attitude is rampant in many developing countries and Western cultures. Too often, donors or leaders from Western countries believe that they need to intervene in less "progressive" countries. Furthermore, leaders in developing countries are often tempted to take this philosophy to the next level by "becoming" the leader that the poor need, many times at the expense of the poor they intended to help. This type of thinking has led to the creation of despots and dictators around the world, destroying any opportunity that the poor might have had to overcome the obstacles set before them.

This problem is compounded by a prevailing inability to create jobs that allow people to make a living in developing countries. Due to fast-growing populations, rural households struggle to grow enough food, as there is less acreage per household. Furthermore, land erosion and deforestation have harmed farming production and output levels. Cities throughout the developing world are quickly growing as they accommodate migration from rural communities. Unfortunately, this has led to greater congestion problems, environmental and health issues, and more competition for fewer jobs available (Bowen 1999).

Thus small businesses are frequently a key factor in economic growth and development. Not only do bigger businesses and industries evolve from small businesses, small businesses create employment in and of themselves. When an individual starts a food stand, purchases domestic animals for their eggs or milk, or buys fabric and material to make textiles or crafts, that person is finding ways to make money. Starting a business can offer a chance to climb out of poverty. Rather than wait to find salaried employment or hope to get lucky, these individuals can use their skills and resources to create income-generating activity. No longer do they need to wait for help from an outside force; they can improve their own situations.

The Informal Sector

Unfortunately, most small and micro-sized businesses in developing countries operate outside of the law in what is called the informal sector. This term is often used in two ways. First, it is used to describe illegal operations that are avoiding either taxes or regulation. However, this does not refer only to drugs or criminal activity but rather defines a large group of activities conducted by people who are attempting to make an honest living but are unable or do not know how to follow the rule of law. While it might seem ridiculous that people would opt out of a legal environment that could protect them, the truth is actually very complicated. In many countries, the process of starting and running a business is difficult and burdensome. Bribing officials to make the paperwork pass or move quicker is an unfortunate reality in many places. Furthermore, if one lacks an education or clear property rights, meeting the legal requirements can be nearly impossible. It is difficult enough to overcome the red tape, but imagine filling out the necessary forms if you cannot read or write or have only a rudimentary education. The second type of informal sector refers to businesses that are smaller and less technologically advanced. Frequently, these are single-person businesses (Webster and Fidler 1996). If they do have employees, they are usually family members and not wage earners.

The informal sector plays a surprisingly large role in the economies of developing countries. When one takes a closer look at cities and towns in developing countries, "informal" enterprises appear to be common. These businesses often operate in public markets, as traveling stands, farms, small shops and stalls, and so on. Development specialists have started to highlight the important role that the informal sector serves in job creation and the development of small and medium enterprises. In times of economic recession, they can serve as a "giant sponge, absorbing much of the shock of periodic economic contraction by soaking up excess labor and by providing second incomes to individuals whose real incomes have been eroded by inflation and public spending cutbacks" (Webster and Fidler 1996, 6). Developing countries tend to be dependent upon the export of oil and other commodities. Therefore when prices fall, their economies are hurt and industries have massive jobs cutbacks. Microbusinesses and the informal sector often protect the poor by offering opportunities to generate additional revenue. When laid off, they can put their skills and training to other uses in the informal sector. When employed in jobs that provide too little pay, which is often the case, they can gain extra money by working on the side. Very few become rich by working in the informal sector, but many find ways to put food on the table because of it.

Small Businesses and Combating Poverty

Microbusinesses and the informal sector are instrumental in the war against extreme poverty. Donald Mead of Michigan State University, using surveys of micro and small businesses in Kenya, Swaziland, Botswana, Zimbabwe and Malawi, noted that:

- Net employment in small enterprises in southern Africa grew by roughly 7 percent a year in the 1980s and early 1990s.
- Small enterprises created more than 40 percent of total new jobs in this region during the 1980s.
- Between 75 percent and 80 percent of all new jobs in small enterprises came from new businesses, with the remainder coming from growth in existing microenterprises.
- Each enterprise was small: 20 percent of sample enterprises added a worker or two, but only 1 percent reached ten or more workers.

- Because the total number of microenterprises was so large, even small growth increments created a large number of jobs (1996, 7-8).

Mead concluded that small and micro-sized businesses were a fundamental source of job growth in African countries. Although they lack the umbrella of protection provided by the law, small businesses in this sector serve to create employment for the poor, with up to 80 percent of new employment came from new businesses. Despite the small size of the majority of the businesses, they are a significant portion of the economy and greatly influence economic growth. The benefits of small businesses to an economy are almost innumerable. They are flexible to changes in the economy, have strong economies of scale, and are more adaptive to consumer preferences and demand than large corporations. Policies and programs that can create more small businesses as well as help them grow can have positive repercussions for the entire economies of developing countries.

Struggles of Small Businesses

Small businesses benefit from their size and flexibility. However, while their small scale allows them to be agile and adaptive, it also comes with disadvantages. For instance, they face cost disadvantages relative to larger businesses. Because of their lack of technology, inability to specialize, limited resources and skills, and generally small operations, they are often unable to use economies of scale to their advantage (Ronnas, Sjoberg, and Hemlin 1998). Uncertainty surrounding their business and markets continues to be a crippling factor in the creation and growth of small and micro-sized businesses. Patrick Alila (2001, 18) describes the situation: "On one hand, many small enterprises survive competition from large ones because they operate in small and unstable markets where larger enterprises would not be profitable. On the other hand, the great instability of the markets on which many small enterprises operate is a major hindrance in their development." While it is fortunate that growth and development can arise out of uncertainty, the uncertainty is still a challenge for the microenterprises in this sector. Some examples of areas prone to uncertainty are farming, commodities, and textiles. Many of these segments are dependent upon the weather and market demands. When negative weather events happen or the international market fluctuates, the microbusinesses bear most of consequences.

Small Business and the Need for Capital

Although small businesses do not require vast amounts of start-up capital, they do need money to finance projects and improvements and purchase supplies. Webster and Fidler, in their book *The Informal Sector and Microfinance Institutions in West Africa*, noted that starting a small enterprise can be easy but actually expanding it can require additional funding, skills, and resources. Especially when operating in the informal sector, small businesses face low barriers to entry, and an entrepreneur can simply start a business of his or her choice. But, without access to additional skills or funding to expand, these operations are usually limited to employment of a single individual and minimal revenues. The book goes on to state that much of the financing for microentrepreneurs comes from their personal savings or from family members. However, within months of starting a business, they face funding shortages. Funding is often required for income-producing activities. Purchasing livestock for their eggs or milk is a common example that highlights the need to purchase something in order to make a profit. Unfortunately, chickens and cattle pass away from a variety of causes: predators, thieves, and disease being some of the most prevalent. Additional funding can be required to purchase more livestock or to replace lost animals. Furthermore, capital is routinely necessary in cyclical activities, such as farming. A farmer might need financing to buy seeds each spring in order to produce his harvest each fall. Regrettably, microentrepreneurs struggle to obtain this financing from most traditional financial institutions.

When considering the needs of the poor entrepreneurs, the question that immediately comes to mind is why banks are not meeting this demand. Webster and Fidler (1996, 19) created a small list of some of the common reasons banks do not lend to microentrepreneurs:

- Small size of the transactions
- Lack of collateral
- Inexperience, illiteracy, and lack of numeracy of the borrower
- Physical remoteness of many informal sector enterprises
- Mobility of many informal sector enterprises
- Lack of bookkeeping or an appropriate compliance framework
- General lack of information about the borrower and of predictability surrounding the transaction.

These factors make it difficult for banks to service poor business owners. Very often, their lending practices are difficult to adapt for these borrowers. For instance, "Most need very small loans for short periods and on an almost immediate basis, because investment opportunities arise and fade very quickly for this group. Most prefer to make very small deposits and to withdraw savings frequently" (Webster and Fidler 1996, 22). These types of quick, almost strange transactions make microentrepreneurs hard to work with. Furthermore, they tend to be rural and difficult to reach, which only makes matters worse. Banks are conservative in nature and sensitive to risky lending. The prospect of providing loans to difficult-to-service customers who have no collateral seems unattractive to many financial institutions.

The inability and unwillingness of conventional financial institutions to service the rural poor leaves a large share of the total population in developing countries without modern financial services. A great amount of savings and capital goes unutilized, wasting many potential investment opportunities. Efficiency gains can be made if these underrepresented and underserved parts of the population can be brought into the system. By including the poor in modern financial services, those individuals' savings can be directed to investment opportunities and further lending activity (Webster and Fidler 1996). Banks and communities have much to gain by providing the poor with opportunities to participate in the financial sector. In addition to the many potential benefits of converting the poor into more middle-class consumers, it is also advantageous for the local community to experience the economy growth associated with start-ups, small business expansion, and business development. The savings of the poor can be recycled into additional loans, resulting in increased banking revenues and community development and creating a win-win.

Sadly, the poor and microentrepreneurs rarely have access to sophisticated financial services because they often have to resort to underground lenders. These moneylenders are often criminals and dangerous to work with but, unfortunately, there are very few alternatives. When an emergency arises, the poor are forced to pursue loans wherever they can find them. Dealing with loan sharks rarely has positive outcomes. More often than not, the poor are caught in a downward spiral, having to take additional loans to pay for the outrageous interest on the loans from the underground lenders. M. A. Mannan (1993, 83) describes the situation of small-business owners in developing countries like Bangladesh which survive week to week and struggle to overcome price shocks: "And since these industries do not have any access to bank credit (except Grameen Bank in a few cases) they usually yield to the Shylock-type moneylenders who lend money at a very exorbitant rate of interest (most often more than 60 percent per annum)." The uncertain nature of their industry makes the poor dependent upon market fluctuations and weather phenomena. A single bad year can put them at risk of forever being hooked, unable to escape the trap of criminal moneylenders. And without the legal framework of the banking sector, the poor lack protection from these moneylenders.

Microfinance and Small Business

Microfinance institutions (MFIs) are able to meet the needs of the poor, and they have greater flexibility then banks and other, larger, financial institutions. MFIs are more adaptable to the needs and requirements of the poor. Traditional banks and financial companies are stricter in their actions and requirements. Developed over centuries of operating, banks have become narrowly focused on their preferred clientele and types of services. Even when they try to adjust their operations to reach a new clientele, their success is very limited. However, microfinance institutions are, by nature, more agile. They have concentrated their practices on the needs of the poor. They can adjust different parts of their lending practices, operate in extensive geographic locations, lend smaller amounts, take more risk with their clientele and not require as much collateral on loans, and so on. These differences allow them to better serve the poor and utilize the opportunities available in that market. Furthermore, because of their smaller size, they tend to have a better connection with the community and therefore are able to meet the individual needs of microentrepreneurs.

CHAPTER 3

INTRODUCTION TO MICROFINANCE

The World of Microfinance

M icrofinance is a set of tools that have been created to provide the poorest of the poor with a method of improving their economic situation. The core of microfinance, microcredit or microloans, is small loans made available to poor individuals who wish to start or grow small businesses. An economics professor in Bangladesh created this concept when he was looking for a solution to help the poor in his home country. Years later, his idea would revolutionize the way the world thought about combating poverty. He believed that it was possible to end poverty in our lifetime. To achieve this dream, he created Grameen Bank (GB), which would provide loans to the poor to start or grow their tiny businesses. The mission of the bank was to serve as a social business—a business devoted to using profits to improve its community. In his book *Banker to the poor: Micro-lending and the battle against world poverty*, he describes his criteria for providing microloans with six standards:

- Loans last one year.
- Installments are paid weekly.
- Repayment starts one week after the loan.
- The interest rate is 20 percent.
- Repayment amounts to 2 percent of the loan amount per week for fifty weeks.
- Interest payments amount to 2 taka per week for every 1,000 taka of the loan (1999, 69).

These simple standards allow the bank to give loans to individuals without an education or understanding of modern finance. GB often provides loans to groups in order to increase accountability, encourage proper use of the loan, and support community development. Groups show ownership of the process and ensure that the loans are spent in an effective manner. This decreases the role of GB and empowers the women and men involved in the practice. Furthermore, it has been discovered that women in poor rural communities have the least access to financial services; therefore, many Microfinance Institutions (MFIs) place a strong emphasis on assisting women (Webster and Fidler 1996, 24). Not only do they have a higher repayment rate than men, when banks provide microcredit to women, the money is more likely to be saved and benefit the entire family (see Ledgerwood 1999; Srinivasan 2010).

Since the creation of microcredit, women have been a focal point of the development program. Originally ignored by mainstream development efforts, women have moved toward prominence in development priorities. This is chiefly because of their importance in combating poverty. As a matter of fact, "women constitute approximately 50 percent of the world's working population, and do roughly 67 percent of the world's work, [yet] they earn only 10 percent of the world's wages, and hold 1 percent of its wealth" (Ringmar 2006, 23). Often, cultural traditions, particularly in many developing countries, view women as second-class citizens. This holds back many poverty-fighting efforts from fully reaching their potential and changing the lives of hundreds of millions of women around the world. Although they tend to do most of the housework, raise children, and work jobs to bring in additional income, women rarely reap the benefits. However, researchers have found that when poverty efforts, such as microfinance, are aimed at women, they tend to have a greater impact on the household. Men are often more risky and selfish with their incomes; women are more likely to use additional income to educate and clothe their children, improve their homes, and save (Webster 1996, 24). Therefore, women are a critical part of the poverty puzzle. Not only do they make up the majority of poor, they are also an integral part of utilizing poverty fighting tools effectively.

The theory behind microcredit is that a microfinance institution provides a small loan to an individual or a group, enabling the person or group to grow or expand a small business. Some examples are a woman purchasing chickens in order to sell their eggs, allowing a man to buy a tool to improve his farming process, helping an elderly woman afford the material needed to sew textiles to be sold, etc. These small, cheap, purchases enable the poor to create income streams, which help them escape clutches of poverty. Microcredit is not, and never was, intended to serve as a complete solution to poverty. Rather, it hoped to be a key piece of the poverty-fighting puzzle. One loan will not immediately bring an individual out of poverty but, it is hoped that, over time and after several loans, the individual will have a constant income.

When Yunus first discussed the idea of microcredit in the 1980s, he surprised policy makers and development experts. At the time, it was believed that the focus of addressing poverty should be toward growing businesses that could hire the poor, to help them obtain salaried employment. However, Yunus fundamentally disagreed with this philosophy. He believed that poverty would be best solved by directing policies and tactics toward the very poor— not by indirectly impacting them through encouraging companies to hire them. He wanted to lend money directly to the poorest of the poor, believing that they could use this money to improve their economic condition (Yunus 1999). Even now, there is a lack of trust that the poor know how to properly manage their finances and effectively use a loan. For instance, they are unable to receive loans from many traditional institutions because they do not have credit histories or collateral. Grameen Bank and other MFIs understand this risk but still provide microloans to poor.

The fundamental difference between microlending and the majority of aid, both private and public, is the approach taken to helping the poor. Most foreign aid and NGO activity can be described as giving free help, hoping that it will provide enough bounce to jump the poor out of poverty. This strategy is simply a handout with great intentions, but it does not materialize into quantifiable and long-lasting results. To counter this flawed reasoning, Yunus created the approach of microfinance, hoping that it would give the poor the tools they need to climb out of the poverty trap. Expanding upon this idea, Yunus (2007, 115) wrote: "In general, I am opposed to giveaways and handouts. They take away initiative and responsibility from people. If people know that things can be received 'free,' they tend to spend their energy and skill chasing the 'free' things rather than using the same energy and skill to accomplish things on their own. Handouts encourage dependence rather than self-help and self-confidence." Instead of giving the poor an apparatus to improve their own condition, handouts only give temporary solutions that weaken their ability to move up the economic ladder. Free supplies, food, etc. only ensure dependence. The poor need and deserve a method of improving their situation by their own hard work.

While microcredit is the foundation of the field of microfinance, it is only a piece of the puzzle. Since Yunus founded GB, microfinance has become a world of financial solutions being provided to the poor around the globe. By allowing them to safely save their money, take out loans for constructing homes, receive various types of insurance, start saving for retirement, and so on, the poor are able to receive many of the same services originally offered only to the affluent. It is believed that the richer one is, the easier it is to get rich. Regrettably, this can be true. "Unfortunately and inevitably, while rich people can usually find services tailored to their specific needs, those less fortunate must choose from options that that are more expensive and less well matched to the needs at hand" (Roodman 2012, 16). When one has a higher income, a home as collateral, etc. there are more methods in which one can save, invest, and grow net worth. The extreme poor do not have access to these services. They are often rural and do not have any financial institutions in their immediate area. Because they do not have collateral, they cannot receive loans to improve their businesses or homes. Even if they hide their money around their house, which is often the only option, there is no way for them to safely save their money or grow it by receiving interest. To make matters worse, when something breaks or there is a bad harvest, the poor frequently have to resort to loan sharks and illegal lenders in order to obtain much-needed funds. This starts a downward spiral that turns poverty into a trap.

Savings Accounts

Unlike some mainstream misconceptions, the poor are able to save (Arun and Humle Rutherford 2009, 8). Although it is assumed that the poor are unable to save due to their financial circumstances, they are more predisposed to saving money when they have the funding and means to do so. As reasoned in Rutherford's *The Need to Save* (43), "The great sense of irony of being poor is that you are 'too poor to save, but too poor not to save'—you may not be able to save much, but if you do not save at all you have no way of getting hold of those 'usefully large lump sums' that you so often need. When the poor are not saving, it is rarely the case that they do not want to or need to. More often it is due to the lack of a safe opportunity to save." Whether it is because they are seeking a depository account, a reliable money handler, or method of saving, for many in developing countries there is a very limited access to opportunities to store and save their money. Although saving is immensely important in order to improve one's financial position, many avoid it or do it haphazardly because they lack the means to do it safely and securely.

Nicknamed "the forgotten half of microfinance," savings accounts are just as instrumental to the foundation of microfinance as microcredit and are in even greater demand (Churchill and Frankiewicz 2006, 21). Although some regulatory systems prohibit MFIs from offering savings accounts and mobilizing deposits, policymakers are "coming around" to the concept that savings accounts are immensely important to providing financial services to the poor that could improve their condition (Armendariz and Morduch 2010, 203). Unlike much of Western civilization, which has easy access to banks and other savings institutions, the rural poor lack a safe way to save their money. They do not have any nearby banks or depositories and cannot afford the related fees. This is a critical problem because savings are an instrumental step in the ability of poor people to improve their economic standing. By saving money, they can gain interest on their accounts, build their funds, and make larger purchases without having to use loans. This saves them money and empowers them to make greater improvements in their personal lives and businesses. If one can save a little money from the annual harvest, after several years he can purchase better equipment without having to borrow money and pay interest. This simple tool is incredibly important and, without an institution willing to provide cheap and safe saving services, the poor are forced to save by hiding their money in their homes, which is less safe, undependable, and impossible for long-term saving. When MFIs provide saving accounts for the poor, it opens the door for economic self-improvement.

Housing Finance

A wonderful example of the innovations being made in the world of microfinance is the offering of housing loans to the very poor. Unfortunately, the vast majority of the world's poor do not qualify for traditional mortgages for even the cheapest commercial and residential buildings. The number of household in the developing world that can actually receive a mortgage is around 20 percent, but regularly as low as 10 percent (Daphnis and Ferguson 2004, 16). To address this issue, MFIs in countries like Mexico offer loans that fit the needs of the poor wishing to purchase property. Unlike microcredit, housing loans are typically larger, made against the collateral of the individual's property, and have lower interest rates (Srinivasan 2010, 49). Additionally, while microcredit often provides funds in one lump sum, housing microfinance provides funds for home repairs or construction, using an incremental lending approach that is more convenient and resembles the timeline and process used by the poor (Goldberg and Palladini 2010, 67). Traditional housing finance providers are often more stringent in their practices and requirements toward borrowers. They typically have stricter requirements defining property ownership, more complex paperwork, and limits for how the funds can be used. This is often a major hurdle for the very poor because they lack reading and writing skills, do not understand complex banking practices and paperwork, and are unable to provide the necessary paperwork to establish property rights.

Much of the world's very poor are rural and have either inherited their property or have squatters rights, meaning that they found unoccupied land have and claimed it by living on it. Once they assume ownership of the land, they typically construct their homes over many years, starting with structures that are haphazardly built and improving them to eventually have concrete walls and roofs (Daphnis and Ferguson 2004, 16-17). This causes legal confusion concerning the legitimacy of their property rights and can prohibit them from using their land as collateral. Banks and traditional financial institutions typically ignore the rural poor for this reason; they require more work and do not provide large amounts of revenue. Microfinance Institutions have started addressing this issue by helping the rural poor establish property rights and devising a system of housing microfinance that has less severe proof-of-title requirements and is more flexible in its approach to lending to the poor. Moreover, unlike traditional lending institutions, housing microfinance "can finance the land acquisition, new home construction, purchase of a complete house, home improvement, construction of additional rooms or other structures (new bedrooms, a garage, or a workshop), home repair and maintenance, and new or upgraded infrastructure (Goldberg and Palladini 2010, 67)." Housing microfinance allows the poor to make necessary improvements to their living conditions and begin to climb out of the poverty trap. This is a service that has largely ignored the very poor until now. By receiving housing microfinance, the poor can improve their quality of life, have safer environments where their children can grow and live, and increase their incomes. Improving their homes and property allows them to grow their collateral, enabling them to qualify for larger loans in the future.

Homeownership is accepted as a strong indicator of future economic growth and prosperity. In the United States, many Americans use the equity on their homes to receive additional capital, as a method of saving for retirement, and to increase their net worth. Along with a strong education system and systemically low unemployment rates, home ownership is one of the "three pillars" of the middle class in industrialized countries (Daphnis and Ferguson 2004, 28). Not only does home ownership lead to more stable families, it is usually associated with a high quality of living, and it can also be used to finance start-ups and small businesses. Entrepreneurs can use the equity on their homes, as many Americans do, to finance projects or capital improvements to their businesses, allowing for further growth and business expansion.

To make housing microfinance even more convenient for the very poor, MFIs have included more in-depth technical assistance as part of loan agreements. For example, the MFI will include "help in the design for improving the quality of the building, meeting pre-loan inspections, lowering the costs for appropriate construction materials, and complying with postloan inspections (Goldberg and Palladini 2010, 68-69)." This assistance is very beneficial to customers; it helps them lower their costs and increases their likelihood of fully repaying their loans. The process and paperwork of building a home and receiving a loan can be very burdensome and frustrating. This problem compounds when the individual cannot read and write and has a limited education. By providing basic assistance and advice to ease the experience, the poor will have better homes, save money, and be better customers to the MFI. It certainly is beneficial to the MFI to have customers who have a better understanding of the lending process, are more likely to repay, and will come back for additional, perhaps bigger, loans in the future.

Microinsurance

One the greatest needs of the extreme poor is access to insurance to protect their property, lives, and families. Unfortunately, due to their poverty and geographic location, they are often ignored by financial institutions or suffer from negative assumptions such as the concept that they are too risky or uneducated to use insurance. The poor suffer the most from environmental changes. When there is a bad harvest due to poor weather conditions or natural disaster, it is always the very poor that are hit the hardest. They do not have as many secondary options or back-up plans and are not able to prepare for catastrophes. For the extreme poor, life is an extremely delicate balance, even in the best of times. When disaster strikes, they lack the emergency savings necessary to recover and therefore lose everything they have accumulated. Therefore, microfinance institutions designed programs for those "ignored by mainstream commercial and social insurance schemes" (Churchill 2006, 13), who are unable to protect themselves. Because of their economic standing, limited education, and difficult geographic locations, the very poor are not considered to be prime customers for typical insurance companies.

Regardless of these challenges and risks, MFIs have created a field to address this growing opportunity to help the poor. Providing microinsurance to the very poor enables them to purchase protection for their property, and the MFI can diversify and grow its revenue; a win-win. Microinsurance is defined by Craig Churchill (2006, 12) as "the protection of low-income people against specific perils in exchange for regular premium payments proportionate to the likelihood and cost of the risk involved." By having access to affordable insurance, the very poor can protect their property just like other businesses. Then, when disasters happen, all progress is not lost, and the poor can overcome and continue improving their situations. This adds stability into their lives, limits their exposure to risk, and protects them from lost income.

Due to the complexity of insurance products, MFIs often partner with larger institutions. Goldberg and Palladini (2010, 60) note that "MFIs can play a decisive role in the design, delivery, monitoring, and evaluation of microinsurance products and, ultimately, the scale of coverage of such products. They cannot provide the complete package by themselves, but they make very valuable partners for insurance companies, government agencies, and other actors in the microinsurance chain." The intricate nature of insurance products makes them difficult for small MFIs and nonprofits to manage completely. However, partnerships with larger, more traditional insurance companies can be very beneficial and expand the number of products that the poor can receive. The example of Allianz partnership with the United Nations Development Programme (UNDP) and the Deutsche Gesellschaft für Technische Zusammenarbeit (GTZ) to provide insurance to the poor in India and Indonesia is a great illustration of the potential for teamwork and growth in the world of microinsurance in developing countries (Churchill 2006, 13).

Microfinance is Still Evolving

The world of microfinance is a young and developing field. Over the next ten to twenty years, many new innovations and changes are expected. With the improvement of technology and increasing access to capital, MFIs continue to grow and attempt new services to the poor. While microcredit is the bedrock of microfinance, MFIs are now considering concepts such as micropensions or social pensions—methods to allow the poor to save for retirement, an idea originally thought impossible. With the addition of microfinance investment funds, individuals in developed countries can invest in MFIs and provide much-needed capital, allowing them to grow their operations. The creation of MFI rating agencies could potentially provide oversight and transparency to the loosely regulated world of microfinance. With the establishment of rating agencies and review groups, investors may be more likely to invest in MFIs. Additionally, some microfinance institutions provide clients with the ability to conduct various payment services. For example, some MFIs allow the poor to receive or submit remittance or transfers from family members, friends, or customers who immigrate to or are from another country and wish to send money back (Churchill and Frankiewicz 2006).

Innovation and the addition of technology will play an instrumental role in microfinance for years to come. These changes will lower costs, make operations more efficient, and increase access to capital, which will mean that more services can be provided. Not only will these improvements mean higher revenues for MFIs, they will lead to additional and better quality services to the very poor. When it comes to combating poverty, everything has a compound effect. The more efficient MFIs are, and fewer operating costs MFIs have, the more they can assist the poor.

CHAPTER 4

SUCCESS OF MICROFINANCE

Although foreign aid has yet to prove itself an effective tool in combating poverty, critics of microfinance are quick to focus on the lack of evidence of macroeconomic effects surrounding microfinance. Despite the lack of positive evidence for foreign aid and government intervention, opponents have repeatedly critiqued microfinance for being unable to estimate the macro impact of microcredit. They claim that the lack of significant evidence weakens the case for microfinance. Critics often use personal stories and individual examples to make their argument. However, the majority of evidence surrounding microfinance indicates otherwise. As noted previously, nearly all impact studies find that clients of microfinance schemes are better off and have higher, more reliable incomes than had they not participated at all. It should be noted that microlending is a choice. If microfinance were harmful, it would eventually be bankrupt due to a lack of customers. Microfinance attracts clients because it is the best option available. Its interest rates are lower than those of loan sharks and other financial institutions. MFIs provide services that other banks choose not to, and they have beneficial impacts on their clients. If individuals were unable to repay their microloans and entered a "death spiral," eventually people would stop borrowing. Others would be warned and therefore not borrow. The high repayment rates, such as 95 percent to 99 percent indicate that individuals are able to repay loans. If the debt were too much to handle, one would see evidence. Eventually, people would be unable to repay their loans. Furthermore, studies that have examined the issue repeatedly find that clients are able to grow their incomes and net worth.

With that said, let us examine the evidence around microfinance. Research conducted on microfinance is almost uniformly positive. Although it has been most used in Bangladesh, the success of microfinance is not limited to that country. Kibas studied the role of microcredit on women entrepreneurs in a section of Africa and found positive results. Sharma and Buchenrieder (2002, 231, Table 11.1) conducted a literary analysis of research on microfinance. They compiled a list of eighteen studies and their results. In their analysis, one can easily see the positive or negative impact that microfinance has had on its customers. In almost every study in their breakdown that has a statistically significant outcome, there is a positive conclusion. In only one study was there a negative outcome. However, in that example, they noted that the "average impact on weekly consumption expenditure is largely negative and seldom statistically significantly different from zero" (2002, 231). Therefore, while the outcome is negative, it is not substantially negative and quite often statistically insignificant. In many of these examples, the outcome is mixed or equivocal or there is a statistically insignificant outcome. Nevertheless, the studies reflect an overall positive narrative for microfinance.

Framing the Debate

Before we dive into measuring the success of microfinance, let's answer a simple question: what are the true goals of fighting poverty? Does that sound like a question with an obvious answer? Unfortunately, there seems to be no clear measurement of success when it comes to helping the poor. When examining the success record of microfinance, it's important to first determine what success looks like. Very often, politicians and nonprofits alike claim victory by counting the number of poor that used their services, how many fewer people live on one dollar a day, and so on. Sadly, this does not even come close to interpreting the actual impact that programs have on the billions of individuals struggling around the world. While announcing how many people your organization or agency provided food or water to might look nice on a donor letter or political advertisement, it does not mean that fewer people will need assistance tomorrow. It simply means that more money has been thrown into the abyss that we call "fighting poverty." Every year, governments and individuals donate billions to help the poor around the world—with no identifiable success. If there is any correlation between foreign aid and economic growth, it would appear to the average viewer as a negative correlation. For example, the African continent has been given trillions of dollars over the last century in foreign aid, yet much of the continent is in turmoil and remains poor. Comparatively, much of Asia has long been shunned by Western aid but has achieved rapid levels of economic growth.

What if we used more objective measurements, such as how many people live on one dollar a day, GDP growth, or per capita GDP? Unfortunately, while it draws the readers' or listeners' attention, this arbitrary marker fails to take into account inflation, the cost of living, or level of opportunity that the poor can enjoy. A country can have an incredibly high level of Gross Domestic Profit (GDP) growth or per capita GDP without any impact on the poorest of the poor. For example, County A has one million people with a national GDP of $1 billion; it therefore has a per capita GDP of $1000. Let's say that one individual finds oil on his land and goes from being worth nothing to becoming a billionaire. The oil found leads to $1 billion in additional national output. Now the country has a GDP of $2 billion and a per capita GDP is $2000. Only one individual had his quality of life significantly improved, but, according to the numbers, everyone appears to be better off. If there were nonprofits in County A, they might feel as if they were having an impact if they used only those statistics. Furthermore, GDP is only a formula. While it has its uses, it can be manipulated, and it often fails to provide an accurate picture of the economic situation. The exact definition of Gross Domestic Product is:

Gross Domestic Product = Consumption + Government Expenditures + Investment + Exports - Imports

Therefore, if a country's government spends heavily on infrastructure building or if the nation is a large exporter of oil, there will be a high GDP. To clarify, per capita GDP is simply the total GDP divided by the number of people in that given area or county. Although this is a massive over-simplification of GDP, it illustrates the difficulty of using it to measure poverty.

To better understand the flaws that are inherent in the GDP formula, consider another example: Three countries (X, Y, & Z) have a GDP of $1 billion each. County X, because of some speculation, sees its stock market soar, allowing the richest to make substantial gains with their investments. The net result is the richest gain an extra $10 million to their net wealth. County Y, on the brink of a recession, chooses to spend $10 million on infrastructure in middle class suburban areas in order to "stimulate" its economy. Lastly, County Z begins a poverty-fighting program that leads to a 50 percent reduction in its national poverty. This means that half the individuals with a net worth of a $100 are now worth $1000. In this scenario, since the majority of the population is below the poverty line, the monetary gain is so small ($900 per individual) that its macro impact on the economy is limited. With only ten thousand people helped by this program, it equates to an increase of $9 million to the national economy. If one only examined the gross domestic product of each economy, the evidence would show that countries X & Y are improving the most when, in reality, the poor are not better off in those countries. Instead, the nation with the smallest increase in GDP, less than 1 percent, saw the greatest decrease in poverty. While this analogy is extremely simplistic, it makes the argument that one has to use more than GDP to measure poverty reduction.

One number that is often used by governments and non-governmental organizations (NGOs) is the number of individuals living on a dollar or two dollars a day. This crude figure does not begin to explain the true economic status faced by billions around the world. As a matter of fact, there are four core faults with using this sort of measurement. First, inflation can change the value of a dollar year to year. This makes this statistic irrelevant after a few years of high or negative inflation. Second, the cost of living varies from place to place to such a degree that a number like this would be misleading. While it is extremely difficult to locate someone living on less than a dollar a day in the United States, does that mean there are no poor in the US? Of course there are poor individuals and families in the US; to make such a statement would be ridiculous and insensitive. Furthermore, the cost of living varies greatly around the world. While it is almost guaranteed that a dollar a day is difficult to live on regardless of location, the level of difficulty changes. For instance, living on a dollar a day in rural South Africa is easier than in Italy. Italy has a higher cost of living; one could earn more than a dollar a day yet still live in a comparable level of poverty. Lastly, how does one measure net worth in dollars in societies that do not use paper money or use it rarely? Often, those who are considered the poorest of the poor seldom use money but rather live off of forms of bartering and trading of services. Therefore, it is difficult to equate a dollar a day with a proper understanding of a quality of life. Lastly, for the sake of argument, let us use the example of communes that can be found in the United States and around the world. By any financial estimate, those individuals are poor. Those individuals do not use any form of money, and their way of life might seem minimalistic, but they would argue that it is a higher quality of life then more industrialized cultures. To put it simply, one cannot always attach a monetary figure to quality of life; nor can one use a dollar to express an individual's desire to make money.

Many times, an advertisement for a nonprofit dedicated to fighting poverty includes a statement such as "this many people have been helped with warm blankets, nets to protect against disease carrying insects, and food to eat." Unfortunately, simple numbers of people served fail to give the donor a complete picture of a donation's effectiveness. For instance, ignoring the possibility of a natural disaster, let us assume that 100,000 people are given free food for a year. Excluding some drastic change in economic conditions and *Ceteris Paribus,* all else being equal, it is reasonable to expect that the majority of those people will still continue to need food aid. Furthermore, if conditions change with the impact of a natural disaster or other factor, even more people could need food aid. If this is the case, no matter how many people donate and how much money is raised, it will never be enough. The same argument applies to many other areas, such as mosquito nets, certain health-care supplies, blankets, etc. While those items may temporality improve the quality of life for a number of individuals, eventually those supplies will wear out or run out and leave a growing number of people without help. This is not to say that they are useless or do not play a vital role in combating poverty. Especially in disaster situations, they can provide much-needed immediate aid. However, they often do not serve as a permanent solution to ending poverty.

Income Inequality

Often, the discussion on poverty leads to the subject of income inequality. Many social scientists, political scientists, and development economists look at income inequality as a measurement of the level of opportunity available to the poor. By using methods and models such as the Lorenz Curve[1], they attempt to show that income inequality leads to political inequality and results in the rich being better off while the poor deteriorate. However, when it comes to the debate in developmental economics, this concept should be viewed as irrelevant. Because of the controversial nature of this argument, let me fully explain it. The focus on eliminating income inequality centers on four core arguments:

1. Unequal distributions of wealth arise from an unequal ability to create wealth.
2. Income inequality creates an unfair system.
3. Wealthier individuals in society have an obligation to devote more of their wealth to assisting the poorer members. (In other words: wealth distribution is morally right.)
4. Distributing wealth from richer members of society to poorer members of society makes the poorer members better off.

Income inequality is not (always) the result of differences in ability but rather it is a combination of differences in opportunity and desires. Statistics that attempt to measure income inequality often fail to take into account the desires of the population that have been sampled. As previously written, one cannot always put a monetary figure on quality of life. Some individuals have a stronger desire than others to make money.

---

[1] The Lorenz Curve is an economic model created by Max Lorenz and is used by development economists to represent income distribution in a given population.

To fully explain this point, let's use an example. We will examine two hypothetical, but not so unrealistic, lives: John and Mike. They are both from middle class families in a small town, they attended the same high school, had similar GPAs and test scores, and both their fathers had similar occupations with similar levels of income. After high school, they went to the same state university and found that they had a passion for numbers. Their passion and ability led them to get jobs as accountants at a big-four accounting firm. After a couple years, both were climbing the ladder of success and had gotten married. However, John found that he did not want to spend all of his time and energy as an accountant. The success was not worth the late nights, hard work, and time away from his family; he and his wife wanted to have a child. Therefore, John decided to switch jobs to work at a smaller firm, closer to his wife's hometown. John's wife wanted to go back to her hometown so that she could manage her parents' coffee shop. Meanwhile, Mike was less interested in having children; he desired to climb the corporate ladder and make a name for himself. As a matter of fact, his wife was the same way. Although she worked in a different industry, she dreamed of being the CEO of her own company. Fast forward to the future, both Mike and John are in their fifties. Mike and his wife are in executive leadership at their respective companies, while John and his wife are working at places that allow them to spend more time with their children. Would one expect their incomes to be the same? It would be ridiculous to expect them to have equal levels of income despite different personal goals, ambitions, and work ethics. Two individuals can have identical backgrounds, skills, and opportunities, yet have very different levels of wealth. Furthermore, although they do not make the same amount of money, it would be foolish to believe that their quality of life should be viewed as unequal. Both parties have met their goals, achieved their dreams, worked at jobs they enjoyed, and married people that they love. If you included those two in a study on income inequality, the results would portray vast inequality. However, the study would fail to capture an accurate picture of the situation.

In the second scenario, let us examine a different story. Ruth and Anna could not be any more different. Ruth is from a low-income, single-parent household in a poor part of town. Anna is from a wealthy suburban home. Both did relatively well in high school, and they were able to go to the same public college. While there, Ruth had to get a job and work as many shifts as she could to afford her education. With this burden, Ruth spent her limited amount of free time studying instead of focusing on distractions like college parties. Anna had no such troubles because her family could afford to pay for her education and, therefore, she dedicated her time to making memories and spending time with friends at the parties Ruth could not attend. As a result, Ruth earned better grades than Anna, even though they both had the same business school classes. After their college educations, both were able to find jobs at the same big-name accounting firm. Ruth was hired because of her grades and work experience. Anna was hired because one of her parents had a connection in the human resources department. Ruth was determined not to struggle financially and dedicated herself to working hard at her job. She spent her time outside of work taking classes and broadening her skills. She finished tasks on time and delivered quality results. Anna did not have the same focus and took her job for granted. Instead of finishing tasks ahead of time, she left work to have drinks with friends. Regardless of the size of her to-do list, she did not mind chatting with coworkers or watching funny movie clips on the Internet. After a couple of years, when the firm had higher positions open, Ruth was an easy candidate for promotion, while Anna would later be replaced with someone who delivered better work and would accept a lower wage. If you had to predict Ruth and Anna's incomes in the future, how would they compare? Would you be shocked if Ruth made more money than Anna? Of course you wouldn't.

To fully examine this point, let's look at one more instance
of income inequality. Charles and James are from a hypothetical
big town in the US Charles was born on the east side in a low-
income household. James was fortunate to be raised in a more
upper middle class household on the west side. Charles's parents
tried their best to put food on the table but struggled between
employment layoffs and paying ever-increasing bills. James was
able to attend a relatively nice school and would later be able to go
to a decent college. In college, he would specialize in engineering,
receive a job after he graduated, and live quite comfortably the
rest of his life. Charles would have a more difficult time. He would
have to drop out of high school his junior year so that he could
get a job to support his family. Years later, between two part-time
jobs, he would receive his GED and take night classes at the local
tech school. Once he received his associate degree as a mechanic,
he could work on automobiles, which offered much higher pay
than any other work he could find. Because he was forced to find
work instead of focusing on his education or other activities, he
would never learn how to manage a budget, utilize services at a
bank, find the right loan, etc. These limitations could mean that
he would pay higher rates of interest on a loan than others, not be
able to take advantage of various benefits at banks and financial
institutions, have fewer options to save for major expenses, and that
saving for retirement would be more difficult, and so on. While
James was able to learn valuable lessons about finances from college
courses and his parents, Charles was not as "lucky." Charles could
eventually find a stable job, save money, and earn a sizable, stable
financial income, but it is unlikely that he would be able to achieve
the same financial well-being as James.

What do these three examples have in common? They reflect
the theory that the level of income depends upon a combination of
opportunity and willingness to utilize the options given to them.
It would be ineffective to use the hypothetical characters in these

examples as subjects in a survey on income inequality distribution. They all have unequal levels of income but for different reasons. Ruth and Mike were able to achieve high levels of financial income by working hard to maximize the chances given to them despite different backgrounds. As a final point, let us examine the first two examples, then compare them with the third. Ruth and Mike had drastically different backgrounds. One was born poor and one was born rich. However, theoretically both achieved similar levels of financial well-being. If the promoters of combating income inequality were correct, we would expect Anna to be the most well off financially; Mike, James, and John to be tied; and Charles to be the worst off. However, in this theoretical comparison, that is not the result. All of this is meant to properly explain the argument that income inequality can be an ineffective and an unhelpful indicator of prosperity and opportunity. It begs the question: since not every individual has the same financial goals, why would researchers be surprised that income would be unequal?

Wealth, in and of itself, does not cause an unfair system. Often, income inequality is associated with bribing politicians and political campaign donations, corporations bending the rules, and companies becoming monopolies. These outcomes are not the result of unequal levels of wealth but of the form of government. In the United States, money can be spent on elections to make advertisements, organize volunteers to talk to voters, and so on. However, it cannot make ballot decisions. Simply put, money cannot vote. Therefore, elections are only as effective as the public is engaged. If the populace researches the candidates, makes decisions based upon facts, and votes, money has no impact on elections. If the public does not make a thoughtful choice, does not vote, etc. then failure can already be predicted, regardless of unequal wealth.

Focusing On Opportunity

Therefore, it is my position that the focus of poverty fighting and economic development should be on increasing opportunity for the poor, rather than on achieving equal levels of financial well-being or measuring it in terms of the number of individuals assisted. When looking at the issues surrounding methods to combating poverty, it is important to have goals and values in mind in order to measure effectiveness. As discussed when examining three different comparisons of financial well-being, not all individuals measure quality of life by levels of income. Therefore, they often take different routes to achieve different goals. It would be ineffective to simply measure incomes and then argue that one is experiencing a better life because he or she makes more money. Rather, when comparing two individuals, one should examine whether the individuals have the opportunity to achieve their economic goals. Measurements of income equality or the number of individuals assisted may not always portray accurate signs of political, regulatory, societal, or discriminatory barriers preventing certain individuals from progressing in a community. For example, let us use a hypothetical example of a nonprofit providing free housing to low-income individuals in a rural village. If the nonprofit only measured success by the number of individuals given housing, it would not account for the number of people who needed housing; nor would it measure whether those individuals who received housing assistance were ever able to achieve self-sufficiency. As a matter of fact, by measuring success as the number of individuals assisted, that nonprofit would have an incentive to never promote self-sufficiency but rather take steps to encourage individuals to continue utilizing assistance—in order to continue to show high numbers. Instead, it would be effective, when examining the program's usefulness, to ask: does the program provide an increase in opportunity for participants that is worth the amount of money spent upon it?

The last part of that question is critical to the concept as a whole. There is a common expression that "the road to hell is paved with good intentions." Very often in social services and efforts to assist the needy, organizations and agencies get distracted with the needs of the people that they are helping and miss more effective strategies or methods to assist them. In the private sector, businesses have to constantly focus upon the cheapest, most efficient way to deliver services or a product. Since their goal is profit, they need to consistently cut costs while increasing their customer base. However, nonprofits do not have the same drive for profits and, therefore, often are not as efficient at cutting costs and improving services. Donors often use research to determine how much of a donation will actually reach the intended recipient instead of being swallowed up by bloated bureaucracies, further fundraising efforts, excessive salaries, etc.

Thus the wording at the end of the question is imperative: "worth the amount of money spent upon it." In other words, is there a way that the same amount could be spent in another format that would allow it to have a better impact? Opportunity costs are an important lesson in economics—there is no such thing as a free lunch! Every penny spent or each second used can no longer be given for another cause. For example, if a government donates $10 million to provide housing to the poor, that is $10 million that cannot be used to provide food assistance. Furthermore, it is illogical for an NGO or government agency to spend millions on fighting poverty every year if the results are only minimal improvements in people's standard of living. If a government spent $1 million fighting poverty but only ten thousand people saw an improvement of ten dollars each to their income, was it worth it? Dollar for dollar, it would be more effective if the government simply wrote a check of a hundred dollars to each of those individuals. If a NGO spent $50 million annually on providing food to the rural poor, but after five years, the same number of people still needed aid, was the NGO's mission a success? It is imperative that poverty-fighting efforts become smarter; those in need, donors, taxpayers, and those providing the serves deserve it. Simply writing blank checks to various causes without finding better methods of giving means that more money is thrown down the abyss—while those in need still have to worry about their future.

With the said, one will notice that in this book, the entire picture of microfinance and its record is examined. Every indicator mentioned has been referenced throughout the chapters. Furthermore, in each indicator, the evidence portrays a similar story of success. Therefore, while some measurements are stronger than others, microfinance can have a positive impact by any standard. While researchers might argue that microfinance and microlending are helpful in combating poverty, it is important to examine why it works. In the words of Tazul Islam (2007, 5): "Poverty alleviation is not just about the quantity of clients reached. It is also about discerning the quality and range of financial services that meets the needs and desires of the poor." Combating poverty is far more about having a strong, positive impact rather than lightly assisting millions of individuals. While microcredit is an instrumental part of microfinance, it is not the entirety of it. The poor, to escape poverty, need access to a wide range of services. The ability to save, borrow money, receive insurance, etc. all have powerful impacts on those attempting to improve their condition. For the average individual in the United States, banking is an aspect of everyday life. It is hard to imagine life without a mortgage, student loans, credit and debit cards, savings accounts, retirement accounts, auto and home insurance, and so on. However, for the extreme poor, those features are not available. The ability to improve one's condition is almost impossible without access to financial services. That's where microfinance comes in. While microlending can hardly be considered a panacea for combating poverty, it can be a powerful force for empowering individuals to overcome poverty on their own (Remenyi 2014, 53). By providing access to different financial services, the poor can invest and grow their small earnings, save small amounts for bigger purchases, and have insurance to protect their livelihoods, all of which help them improve their ability to grow their income and protect their earnings. Unlike many other forms of poverty alleviation, MFIs make revenues by giving services to the poor. Most MFIs are profit-seeking, or at least they make profits with the intentions of using them to provide further services to the poor. Additionally, the services they deliver enable the poor to improve their own circumstances rather than rely upon someone else's assistance. Instead of waiting in a line for food or water, they are treated with respect like any other responsible customer.

Furthermore, much of the focus of microfinance goes toward microlending, which gives small loans to individuals that are starting or growing their businesses. As discussed previously, these are often people who simply need to purchase supplies for their textile-making or livestock to sell their milk or eggs. While these businesses are small and frequently employ one or two people, they are critical to the local and national economy. The fact is that these businesses create wealth, which would otherwise not exist (Kloppenburg 2006). It provides incomes to the extreme poor by utilizing their unique skills, knowledge, or resources. Small businesses can evolve into larger businesses, creating jobs for the surrounding community. Furthermore, development breeds development, and growth creates more growth. When individuals receive loans that grow their businesses, they can use that growth to increase their incomes. Bigger incomes can be reinvested into their businesses. Higher income is used to purchase products from the surrounding area. It can buy livestock from neighbors, construction supplies, hire employees, and so on. Higher income for one business can mean that the community receives additional revenues. While the microloan is intended to help an individual, the effects are felt throughout the area. Even though microloans are small, often only a few dollars at a time, each takes a small step in the right direction. Each microloan helps individuals improve their circumstances. Repeated microloans can eventually make a big impact. Not only do they make small improvements each time, they build credit history and can enable the individual to receive higher amounts of credit. Microloans were never intended to eradicate poverty in a single attempt. Critics of MFIs often make the wrong assumption and measure success by a single microloan. The goal of microlending is to solve poverty by empowering individuals, little by little, to overcome poverty.

CHAPTER 5

THE PROBLEM OF INTEREST RATES

Since Mohammad Yunus first conceived microfinance in his effort to address poverty in Bangladesh, certain aspects of its methodology have come under scrutiny. Specifically, the issue of charging high rates of interest on small loans to poor individuals that one is intending to aid is arguably the most controversial part of the concept. With millions of people on five continents relying upon microloans to improve their businesses and living conditions, microfinance has moved to the forefront of modern discussions on fighting poverty. This chapter will examine critics' claims concerning the rates of interest charged by MFIs. The leading argument among microloan opponents is that high rates of interest charged by MFIs create a downward spiral for the borrowers. Their reasoning is that borrowers are very poor and often take microloans in an emergency and do not understand the consequences. Therefore, when the time comes to repay the loans, they must borrow more because they lack the money to pay the lenders. This circle of borrowing to pay off loans sends the poor into worse poverty, destroying their chances of improving their condition.

This argument is countered by the argument that high rates of interest charged in microloans not only avoid such negative outcomes, they also allow lending institutions to expand their services and outreach, contributing to aiding more people and an overall reduction in poverty. By using recent and relevant data on the subject, it's possible to gain a better understanding of the importance of interest rates in microlending.

Yunus's hope was that, in gaining access to very small loans, often only a few dollars, the poorest of the poor could invest in improvements to their businesses, grow their incomes, and began to move up the economic ladder. With these loans, individuals could buy supplies, make infrastructure improvements, or purchase tools. Perhaps the most intriguing part of the process is that many microlenders have emphasized women in their outreach due to their potential to raise whole families out of poverty through a willingness to invest in their children's educations and their higher rates of return on loans (Webster and Fidler 1996). MFIs have argued that this strategy has allowed many women to improve their socio-economic standing and has reduced poverty in many third-world countries. Despite these claims, some remain unconvinced. Particularly in recent years, some have come forward with research and stories reflecting the potential hazards of microfinance. Many of the leading arguments against microlending concern the interest rates that are being charged. With rates often in the double digits and much higher than commercial banking rates, microloans are viewed as exploitative and an attempt to profit off the poor.

Conversely, my research on the subject leads me to believe that interest rates charged in microloans avoid the undesirable consequences previously mentioned and enable lending institutions to grow their amenities and expand outreach, allowing for more people to be assisted and an overall lessening of poverty.

While it is true that there are only roughly ten thousand or so microfinance producers, of which only two hundred or so are profitable, the market potential is considerable. Four hundred million clients internationally currently lack access to financial services and potentially could be aided by microfinance institutions (Matthäus-Maier and Von Pischke 2008, VIII). For many reasons, Mohammad Yunus and his concept of microlending have forever changed the modern field of finance. Now there is a growing field of financial institutions that charge interest rates independent of government actions (excluding usury laws and similar regulations) and act on a free market supply and demand approach. Furthermore, these institutions are not based in major urban areas or traditional financial districts but focus their services in rural and inner-city environments, reaching a clientele that, until recently, was largely excluded from participating in financial services and practices.

Because of their recent creation, "one might best describe the environment in which many of them have operated as 'legal limbo'" (Drake and Christen 2002, 16-17). Since they do not adhere to the same parameters many larger banks uphold, some governments have been conflicted on how to regulate them. Some national and local governments have passed strict laws concerning microfinance, while others choose to avoid examining the subject too carefully. Thus many microfinance institutions operate in a gray area as to their legality and legal rights. One particular aspect of this gray area concerns usury laws and the rates of interest charged by lending groups. Although some microfinance institutions do not face difficulties concerning their interest rates, governments are increasingly contemplating placing restrictions on interest rates being charged.

Critics of microlending dispute the advantages claimed by MFIs and assert that the negative implications of microloans mitigate any positive results and have caused a worsening of the conditions for borrowers. While their arguments are not limited to the subject of interest rates charged by microlenders, interest rates are certainly a main focus and a foundation to many harmful allegations concerning microfinance. Though some have questioned the philosophical nature of charging the poor interest, the most common argument against microloans follows the line of logic that forcing borrowers to repay loans with interest prevents them from saving their money and escaping poverty. In cases where individuals request loans to pay for running expenses, emergencies, or other non-income generating activity, the argument follows, when it becomes time to make payments on the loans, borrowers have to either sell their belongings, have their children work, or obtain another loan from a different institution or loan shark. Regardless of which option they choose, the borrowers and their families are hurt by the outcome. Therefore, microloans become a form of imprisonment or trap that prevents people from ever escaping poverty (Bateman 2010).

Because of these criticisms, politicians in many developing countries have either passed legislation regulating interest rates or are actively considering such legislation. Governments have two common methods of reducing interest rates on microcredit. The first method, subsidizing the lenders, is not often used because it is opposed in the microfinance community. Many microfinance institutions reject government funding due to their desire to remain independent, flexible, and self-reliant. Any government subsidy could be followed with new parameters, a loss of personal discretion, and unreliable funding. The second approach of mandating an interest rate ceiling is far more popular among the public. However, the task of abstractly determining acceptable interest rates is difficult, if not impossible (Torre and Vento 2006, 50). Limits on interest to protect borrowers from abusive rates often have disastrous consequences. Advocates for microfinance often criticize price controls because they tend to hurt rather than aid poor entrepreneurs by "rationing credit artificially" (Goldberg and Palladini 2010, 46). They make it difficult, if not impossible, for firms to cover their costs, causing them to remove themselves from the market or avoid entering altogether. This either denies possible borrowers access to financial aid or forces them to resort to informal lenders who charge higher rates and use more abusive tactics. Furthermore, caps on interest rates may result in less transparency about the actual cost of borrowing because lenders often compensate for decreased earnings with confusing fees (Goldberg and Palladini 2010). MFIs focus on simple and efficient operations to function in tough markets. But when governments intervene, MFIs are forced to find alternative means of funding. These alternatives are more confusing for borrowers to understand and cause additional fees to make up for funding shortages. Although governments may have the best of intentions, the poor often are worse off. Because of the cost structure of microfinance firms, interest rates are the main funding mechanism that enables them to operate competitively and efficiently. Restrictions rarely achieve their stated purpose of protecting endangered members of the populace. If they do not force firms to use alternative fees or force them out entirely, they drive lenders into the informal sector, where poor borrowers are no longer able to benefit from legal protections and the originally envisioned structure of the low-cost services (Ledgerwood 1999).

Additional studies done on the subject of microcredit interest rates refute the argument that they are abusive or harmful to the goals of poverty reduction. Rosenberg, Gonzalez, and Narain (2009, 175) found that, "Based on 34 reports from 21 countries, MFI rates were almost always lower—usually vastly lower—than rates charged by informal lenders." In the world of extreme poverty, those in need of a loan often face two options: resorting to an informal lender or an MFI. In a perfect world, the poor would have access to a mainstream bank with much lower interest rates, but that is not always a possibility. The reason for the creation and expansion of microcredit is the lack of action and assistance from banks and other financial institutions. Therefore, when critics argue against microlending, they often ignore the lack of alternatives for the poor. That is why the regulation of interest rates is harmful. Caps on interest rates of MFIs can hurt low-income borrowers because they force MFIs to limit or withdraw completely from the field and then the poor lose access to lending alternatives (Rosenberg 2008).

The critics' opposition to microfinance is not only unfounded, it is harmful to the poor. At a minimum, the extreme poor should have the right to choose financial services that are offered to them. Instead of being limited in their options, the poor deserve access to the same services that the wealthy enjoy. If there are firms willing to provide loans to the poor, many of whom have no credit history and are difficult to serve, and the poor desire those services, the options should be available. Microfinance centers on the premise of choice: the poor have the opportunity to choose the same financial services that most others utilize on a regular basis. It is a willful choice to use a microfinance institution. The poor are not forced or coerced. Rather, the poor are able to access services that previously have been unavailable. The alternative to microfinance is dangerous. If governments and nonprofits discourage MFIs, the poor have fewer options. Many times, the only other option is loan sharks who charge higher rates of interest and are more dangerous to work with.

Furthermore, if microlending were truly harmful, one would see a reduction in the number of borrowers requesting it. The poor borrow from MFIs because they are the best alternative from their perspective. If the interest rates were higher than other lenders or the costs were more, the poor would merely pursue other options and not request a loan from an MFI (Goldberg and Palladini 2010).

Although critics are quick to point to the downside of interest rates, they rarely mention the reason for high interest rates. They immediately assume that microfinance institutions charge exorbitant rates out of greed and to have high earnings. However, the evidence does not reflect this argument. Goldberg and Palladini (2010, 48) found that the rates generally reflect MFIs' high costs of business, not their level of greed, remarking, "Evidence suggests, however, that MFIs are not profiting excessively or charging their borrowers inappropriately high rates." According to financial data, most MFIs in their research only had a rate of return on capital of 1.1 percent (2010, 43). MFIs tend to charge higher rates of interest than banks because of the expensive nature of their lending practices; their customers are often rural and hard to reach and their lack of collateral and credit history entails higher levels of risk (Webster and Fidler 1996). It is naïve to assume that they can provide the same quality of service and not need to increase the rates of interest. If lending to the extreme poor were easy and profitable, the mainstream financial sector would already be participating.

One might easily assume the solution to high interest rates is to provide subsidies or financial assistance to microfinance institutions. Since their interest rates are the result of their high cost structure, subsidies might allow them to lower rates and remain profitable. Unfortunately, it is not that easy. For starters, MFIs are financially self-sufficient and sustainable. Although they must charge high interest rates, their practices tend to be efficient enough to survive and grow in new and risky sectors. In this context the term *self-sufficient* or *sustainable* can be understood "as a ratio of adjusted operating revenues to adjusted operating expenses (financial, administrative, provisions), where the adjustments show whether or not the institution could cover its costs if its activities were unsubsidized and if it had to raise capital at commercial rates" (Balkenhol 2007, 4). Therefore, when this paper refers to MFIs as sustainable or self-sufficient, it is saying that the MFI is not dependent upon donations or government assistance. It may receive them to make improvements or expand operations, but it does not require them to exist.

MFIs started as NGOs and nonprofits relying upon donations from around the world to support their operations. However, some institutions have moved beyond the donation level to become self-sufficient. Their high rates of return and efficient practices enable them to be free of fundraising and allow them to focus more upon their services. A fundamental method of measuring success of a lending institution is to view repayment rates as a representation of their return on investment (ROI) (Webster and Fidler 1996). If repayment rates are low, then it can be understood that microcredit either cannot create enough income-generating activity for the borrower to be able to repay or that credit interest is so burdensome that borrowers cannot afford it. However, if repayment rates are high, then it can be assumed that borrowers are able to afford to repay the loans, with interest, and not be severely harmed by the practice. Most MFIs have incredibly high repayment rates, regularly over 98 percent. For instance, Hope International, one of the largest MFIs, boasts a repayment rate of 98 percent (HOPE international 2016). Furthermore, it is agreed that repayment rates lower than 95 percent are dangerous and discouraged (Webster and Fidler 1996). Because of their cost structure, MFIs require a higher repayment rate despite their high interest rates. To stay profitable, MFIs need to balance high interest rates with high repayment rates. MFIs cannot afford to charge interest that is burdensome to the point of being unaffordable. They must also charge interest rates high enough to fully fund their practices. Therefore, the high levels of repayment further speak to the success of microlending. If microlending were harmful or caused a debt spiral, evidence would appear in the form of lower rates of repayment.

The repayment rates and ability to be self-sufficient have almost been immune to the Great Recession and global market troubles. While most banks were hurting after the credit crisis and slowdown of the world economy, MFIs were barely impacted, and most grew despite these challenges. This is partly due to the steady innovation and alternative approaches of MFIs. While the financial sector is regarded for its immunity to change and its steady practices, MFIs have found new and more flexible methods of serving clients. For example, the South Indian Federation of Fisherman Societies (SIFFS) provides various services to small-scale fish workers. One of its services, microlending, has made changes to its program to provide borrowers with flexibility in repayment. Srinivasan (2010,

41), describes the practice: "A loan of 12 monthly installments is repayable in 14 months and a loan with 36 monthly installments is repayable in 42 months. This flexibility has been built because the lean and off-seasons would not produce income flows to meet the monthly loan repayments in full." Because poor entrepreneurs often have cyclical or seasonal periods of revenue, typical repayment schemes do not always work. By adjusting their practice, SIFFS made it easier for borrowers and increased its lending practice—a win-win.

The examples and stories of successes in microfinance are innumerable. During political and financial turmoil in Ecuador, a bank turned its attention away from lending to medium and large businesses toward microenterprises, the action empowered the bank to become Ecuador's most profitable bank. Despite an economic recession, microfinance institutions in the Philippines grew their market share and revenues while traditional banks struggled. While many Indonesian banks shut down or went bankrupt when their country's currency faltered and the country went into a recession, the People's Credit Bank focused on microlending—and kept repayment rates high and grew profits (Kahn and Jansson 2007). These examples highlight the flexibility, dependability, and potential of microfinance institutions. Evidence shows that they can withstand recessions and difficult clientele and geographic regions, and even make it in war-torn and disaster areas. Their ability to grow under adverse circumstances is reliant upon their flexibility and ability to adapt.

To be financially sustainable without the assistance of governments or donations, MFIs focus upon increasing the average loan size in their portfolio, finding investors, and making their organizations more efficient. Like any private-sector company, MFIs utilize modern technology, attempt new services, and try to achieve economies of scale in order to compete, grow profits, expand operations, and help the poor. While this will be discussed in depth later, growing the average loan size and finding investors have become increasingly important to MFIs. With modern investment markets, some MFIs have attempted to grow operations by obtaining credit from other places. Those who want to be a part of the microfinance process can easily invest in a microfinance mutual fund (mutual fund with a portfolio of diverse MFIs) or invest in individual MFIs. Some MFIs specialize in serving as mediators between investors and borrowers. Srinivasan, in his *Microfinance India State of the Sector Report* (2010, 30), writes, "A poll of 50 investment banking firms/companies brought out that microfinance is the top ranked destination for investments in financial sector today. Of those who voted, more than 80 percent rated microfinance as the best sector for investments." Microfinance is a growing part of the financial services sector. Its creation and evolution has created a variety of investment opportunities. This allows investors to receive returns and grow profits, MFIs are enabled to expand their operations, and the poor have greater access to financial services—a win all around.

A simple yet effective way to grow profitability is to increase the average loan size in the portfolio. Larger loans entail lower interest rates and higher repayment amounts. However, this means that loans will have to go to those who are less poor because the extreme poor cannot afford bigger amounts. Therefore, MFIs can balance the riskiness of lending to the extreme poor and the small returns on each of their loans with lending to slightly wealthier clients who require larger loans and are less financially endangered. While this decreases the focus toward helping the extreme poor, it allows MFIs to continue operations in situations where they otherwise might not be able to participate. MFIs are finding innovative ways to overcome high interest rates and assist clients in repaying their loans. With flexible repayment programs, adjusting the average loan size in a portfolio, and seeking investment from outside, MFIs grow, improve and prosper. Because of these innovations, interest rates do not tend to have the burden critics often claim.

Since the inception of microlending in the 1970s, there has been a great deal of research on the impacts of microlending, particularly concerning the subject of interest rates. One of the most common methods has been the use of impact studies of participants. These "before and after" pictures offer an excellent portrayal of the results of microfinance. It should be noted that there are many moving parts and hidden details that impact studies can miss, so they are not a perfect representation of the outcomes of microcredit. Nevertheless, Webster and Fidler (1996, 23) note, "Virtually all show that clients of microfinance programs have higher and more stable incomes than they did prior to their participation." Although this reinforces the argument that interest rates in microloans do not typically have a negative impact, more data should be examined before any conclusion is made.

Kibas, in his study, analyzed three non-governmental organizations (NGOs) conducting microfinance in Uasin Gishu District in Kenya and closely examined the use and impact of those microloans. The organizations that he viewed were K-REP, World Vision, and the Church of the Province of Kenya (CPK). When describing the study's process, he writes that it was conducted by personal interviews with the loan recipients. A sample of 122 microenterprises was selected, with the population size for the study around twelve hundred microenterprises, out of a total estimated population of ten thousand that existed in the geographic area (Kibas 2001, 203-204). Reviewing multiple NGOs in a specific geographic area and examining a certain clientele (women entrepreneurs) strengthens the credibility of the study because it reduces the risk of outside factors having a strong impact on the results.

It is very difficult to achieve a quality study of the impacts of microlending because of the strong potential for other factors to interfere. For instance, measuring the impact on poverty through monetary value before and after some take microloans is like measuring the number of sick people inside a hospital and comparing it to individuals outside of it. People who are in the hospital, or recently were, are more likely to be sick than individuals who have never needed to go to the hospital. The same could be said about those seeking microloans; people who desire microloans are already poor and one or two loans should not be expected to rescue them completely from poverty. With that said, one should not over emphasize microloans' positive impacts because of the built-in advantages that borrowers might have. It is difficult to compare "apples to apples," due to the fact that individuals who request microloans tend to be more entrepreneurial than individuals that do not; therefore, they are more likely to achieve better results. It is arguable that due to their risk-taking nature, they would already have improved outcomes compared with other individuals who self-selected themselves away from obtaining a loan.

Figure 1.

Loan Use	Frequency	Percentage
Business Only	57	46.7
Business and Personal Use	57	46.7
Used to Pay Off Creditors	2	1.6
Other Uses	6	5
Total	122	100

(Kibas 2001, 209, table 9.2)

Chart on Loan Use

When examining Kibas's results, some interesting results come to light. Figure 1 shows how the sample used their loans, with 93.4 percent using their loans for business/business and personal use and less than 2 percent use their loans to repay past loans. While ideally zero percent of individuals would use their microloans to pay off past lenders, nevertheless having a mere 1.6 percent is a positive outcome for advocates of microfinance and refutes previous arguments of a "death spiral" or that debtors would use their credit to repay past lenders instead of improving their situation. One should not be immediately concerned that 46.7 percent of individuals, the same number that only use it for their business, use the funding for both personal and business uses. The reasoning is that in very poor households, the connection between personal property and business property is a gray area. For instance, many microentrepreneurs run their businesses inside their homes or the products that they sell are simply surpluses of clothing or food that they make for their family. Furthermore, using microloans to pay for personal issues may not be a poor use of the loan because borrowers might be spending it on whatever is preventing them from growing their businesses. If the microloan allows them to fix a hole in their roof, repair a fence, or take care of other domestic expenditures, it is very possible that that leads to more productivity or an increase in their ability to focus on their microbusiness.

Figure 2.

Areas of Impact		Effect	On	Enterprises
	Increased	No Change	Decreased	TOTAL
Assets	93 (76.2%)	23 (18.9%)	6 (4.9%)	122 (100%)
Sales	105 (86.1%)	7 (5.7%)	10 (8.2%)	122 (100%)
Profits	107 (87.7%)	6 (4.9%)	9 (7.4%)	122 (100%)
Employment	34 (27.9%)	86 (70.5%)	2 (1.6%)	122 (100%)

(Kibas 2001, 210, table 9.3)

Areas of Impact

Taking a step further, Figure 2 explores the actual impact of the microfinance on the amount of assets, sales, profits, and employment in the businesses sampled. If the hypothesis is correct that high interest rates are not entirely harmful but allow microfinance to grow and have a beneficial impact on the community, then the results should show an increase in the four different sections, with a minimal number of firms seeing decreases in those areas. Kibas's results show a general support of the hypothesis, with employment being less agreeable. Among the four sections, microentrepreneurs saw the biggest increase in sales (86.1 percent) and profits (87.7 percent). These numbers disagree with the view that microloans do not improve profits because they go to emergency expenses and operating expenditures. With only 8.2 percent seeing a decrease in sales and 7.4 percent seeing a decrease in profits, one could contend that the negative results are negligible. Regardless of how effective microcredit can be, some will always have negative outcomes due to unrelated and uncontrollable events.

The increase or decrease in assets is arguably the most important of the four sections because it most accurately reflects the wealth of the borrowers. It is possible that sales and profits for the microbusinesses could increase, while the general well-being of the borrowers decreased, due to the magnitude of the loan or amount of interest. But, because fewer than 5 percent of borrowers saw a reduction in assets, it appears unlikely that individuals had to resort to selling off property or belongings to repay the loans. To the contrary: 76.2 percent of the borrowers in the sample increased the amount of assets that they owned. This means that clients made capital investments in their firms, allowing them to increase future productivity, which resulted in lasting benefits to their microenterprises. This is critical to the argument that microloans have positive impacts on fighting poverty and helping individuals improve their economic conditions. The only aspect that was disappointing is the impact on employment. While fewer than 2 percent of borrowers experienced decreased employment, only 27.9 percent saw an increase in hiring. As discussed previously, Muhammad Yunus never intended for microloans to be centered on increasing employment but instead focused on the well-being of the borrowers. With that said, increasing employment is a very positive side effect of entrepreneurship and combats poverty in the surrounding community.

Figure 3.

How the loan money helped	Frequency (n = 122)	Percentages
Increase in stock	64	52%
Settlement of domestic/personal expenses	20	16%
Purchase (and construction) of fixed assets	12	10%
Business expansion and growth	5	4%
Business sustenance	5	4%
Started/acquired new business	4	3%
Prompted the entrepreneur to work hard	2	2%
Other	1	1%
Loan did not help	9	7%
Total	122	100%

(Kibas 2001, 215, table 9.5)

Chart on How the Money Helped

Figure 3 indicates that microloans actually helped and shows where the money was spent. It is not surprising that the large majority of loans, 52 percent, were invested in business stock, due to the importance of raw materials to many microentrepreneurs. Of the options listed, the most important numbers are the amounts invested in fixed assets (10 percent), business expansion and growth (4 percent) and the starting and acquiring of new businesses (3 percent), because these represent capital investments and income-generating activities. Furthermore, Kibas measured the quality of relationships of the borrowers to see if financial difficulties or debt were having major repercussions on the families, suppliers, or spouses of borrowers, or with the lenders themselves. Kibas (2001, 212) found:

> The relationship between the respondents and others was reported to have generally improved during the loan period. Relationship with customers in particular were said to have become much better by 73 (60%) of the 122 respondents. This was closely followed by relationships with family members 69 (57.5%), suppliers 61 (50%) and spouses 39 (54.2%).

This reinforces the hypothesis that the borrowers are aided by microloans instead of being harmed by high interest rates. The improvements across the board in the borrowers' various relationships highlight the increased financial security that they experience. Borrowers having financial difficulties would immediately begin to show signs of stress and strained relationships, but the study reflects the exact opposite results.

When examined even more closely, no connection is apparent between interest rates and the likelihood of microloans going bad. Joe Remenyi (2014, 56) notes, "In fact, data gathered from most of the major MFIs reported here and in Hulme and Mosley, 1996, shows that there is no apparent statistical relationship between the arrears rate, measured as the percentage of the loan portfolio that is delinquent by six months or more, and the rate of interest charged on loans." Although critics are quick to claim abuse, there is no statistical or actual correlation or connection between the interest rate and the odds of default. When determining interest rates, many factors are considered. MFIs have no intention of charging interest rates that cripple the poor or prevent them from repaying. They understand that they maximize their profits when clients are able to repay their credit and return for another loan. With that said, there are always exceptions. Like any profit-making scheme, some will attempt to use the strategy to make quick money instead of maximizing long-term revenues. However, those are the exception and not the rule.

While the Kibas study reflects positive results of microlending, Rosenberg, Gonzalez and Narain specifically analyzed the role of interest rates in microlending and attempted to verify or correct the different claims made about high interest rates. Critics of high interest charged by microlenders often highlight many microfinance institutions that try to profit off of lending to the poor. However, Rosenberg, Gonzalez and Narain (2009, 172) found that an MFI, at the median level, is able to reduce its interest rate by 17 percent (not 17 percent of the loan amount). As a matter of fact, they went on to conclude, "Completely eliminating all profits would reduce the median MFI's interest rate by only about one-sixth, an effect that is smaller than many people might expect." The amount of profit made by an MFI on each loan is so small that to reduce interest to the point of zero profits would be a miniscule difference. As a matter of fact, due to the cost structure and diseconomies of scale, the highest rates of interest are charged by institutions focused most strongly on their social mission (Cull, Demirgüç-Kunt and Morduch 2009, 18). Despite claims that the high interest rates are charged by greedy profit seekers, in reality the institutions that maintain the strictest social missions limit themselves to the very poor who are riskier and necessitate smaller loans, therefore forcing themselves to require the highest rates of interest. Comparatively, firms with less-strict social missions and that are more focused on profits have the luxury of being able to hedge some risk on slightly wealthier clients who require larger microloans, allowing them to lower their overall rates of interest. Cull, Demirgüç-Kunt and Morduch (2009, 19) went on to find that "Institutions that make the smallest loans on average are also the institutions that face the highest costs per unit lent (a result that holds up to regressions after controlling for institutions' age, inflation, country-level governance, GDP growth, region, and lending method) ... institutions with the highest costs per unit also charge the most to their customers." This logically follows and reinforces the notion that interest rates are not driven by abusive profit seeking but instead are determined by costs. Furthermore, it is important to note that interest rates among microfinance institutions continue to decrease. Since 2003, MFI rates of interest have declined by 2.3 annually, much more than typical bank rates (Rosenberg, Gonzalez and Narain 2009, 175).

Lastly, it is important to note that the very poor have little choice when it comes to financial services. Before microfinance, mainstream banking institutions avoided the poorest of the poor and left them to resort to informal moneylenders, who often charge higher rates of interest and are less flexible. Even if MFIs charge "abusive" rates of interest, they are still more attractive than any available alternative. The difference between informal lenders' interest and microfinance interest is quite substantial, even on a monthly basis. To put it in perspective, informal lenders typically charge nominal effective interest rates of 10 percent to more than 100 percent a month; comparatively, many microfinance institutions charge nominal effective rates between 2 percent and 5 percent per month (Robinson 2009, 50). If one is to compare solutions to poverty to their alternatives, microloans offer an attractive, potentially self-sustaining approach to improving the welfare of the very poor. Without them, it is almost certain that hundreds of millions of poor individuals around the world would be forced to resort to the cruel practices of informal lenders or live without any access to financial services.

While the debate over microfinance's relatively high interest rates is far from over, research done on the subject has shone a positive light on microloans' potential. Studies have reinforced the hypothesis that rates of interest in microlending are not abusive but enable microfinance lenders to develop their services, provide more microloans, and continue to improve the economic situation of the very poor. While it is true that there is no study yet that has attained any consensus as to its dependability (Armendariz and Morduch, 2010), much of the evidence for microlending demonstrates positive results. Furthermore, claims that the interest rates charged are abusive or greedy do not take into consideration the cost of operation and often misunderstand the structure of the firms within the microfinance industry. Attempts to limit interest rates often result in negative outcomes that hurt the poorest of the poor. Studies such as the one by Kibas provide insight into how microloans are used, how they help, and the outcomes of the participant borrowers. These studies reinforce the hypothesis previously discussed and argue for additional expansions of microlending.

CHAPTER 6

FINDING SUCCESS IN BANGLADESH

A lthough microfinance has been attempted around the world, Bangladesh is the poster child of microcredit. If one were to measure the success of microlending and the microfinance industry, it would be best to start at its birthplace. Since its creation in the 1970s, microfinance has taken off and served millions around the world. In 1974, Henry Kissinger described Bangladesh as "a bottomless basket case" (Pollin, Feffer, and Daley-Harris 2007). Sadly, it was. When Bangladesh became independent in 1971, it had "one of the lowest per capita income (less than $100) in the world, a poorly developed industrial sector (4% of GNP for other than small scale and cottage industries), a low literacy rate (around 20%), war-shattered transport, power and other economic infrastructures and, overall, an abject poverty" (Mannan 1993, 19). Mannan (1993, 19) went on to say that 80 percent of the population, roughly 76.39 million, worked as peasants. At the time, it was one of the most destitute nations in the world. It was war-torn, lacked infrastructure, and did not have many notable natural resources. If there was ever a country that needed a plan to address poverty, surely it was Bangladesh.

Since the 1970s, microfinance has blossomed in Bangladesh. Initially, it served forty-two poor individuals; now there are twenty

MFIs in the country and they have twenty-one million clients, impacting 105 million family members in a nation of 140 million people (Pollin, Feffer, and Daley-Harris 2007). Therefore, studying Bangladesh should shed light on whether microloans truly help achieve their stated goals of reducing poverty. To start, one should examine the county's economic improvement as a whole. Here are several core statistics about growth since the birth of microfinance:

- Although the county lost much of its foreign aid, it was able to recover and even grow its economy (Islam 2007, 54).
- Its poverty headcount, as a percentage of the population, was 31.5 percent in 2010, down from 40 percent in 2005 and 48.9 percent in 2000 (World Bank 2016).
- Its life expectancy is now seventy-two years, up from sixty-five in 2000, and above the average of Southern Asia, sixty-eight years (World Bank 2016).
- Although its GDP growth rate was around 4 percent in the 1980s, since 2013 it's been over 6 percent (Yunus and Weber 2007, 106; World Bank 2016).
- The economic growth did not lead to income inequality. The Gini index, often used to measure income inequality and the distribution of wealth, changed from 0.30 in 1995 to 0.31 in 2005, which is a very slight decline. Furthermore, "Since 2000, the real per-capita income of the bottom 10 percent of the population has grown at the same annual rate of the top 10 percent (2.8 percent)" (Yunus and Weber 2007, 106).
- Last, but not least, Bangladesh accomplished its "Millennium Development Goal on gender parity at the primary and secondary educational levels; the fertility rate in Bangladesh has fallen from 6.4 in 1970 to 3.2 in 2004; and the number of deaths of children under five per 1,000 live births has fallen from 239 per thousand in 1970 to 77 in 2004" (Pollin, Feffer, and Daley-Harris 2007).

Despite its relatively slow income growth and poverty reduction leading up to the 2000s, its improvement in human development was much faster and has been called "truly remarkable" (Islam 2007, 53). While poverty remains a major problem for Bangladesh, great gains have been made. Obviously, microcredit is not the only reason for this success but it is a surprisingly significant factor.

A study performed by Shahidur Khandker (Pollin, Feffer, and Daley-Harris 2007), which examined three MFIs that were operating in Bangladesh, concluded that "microcredit accounted for 40% of the entire reduction of moderate poverty in rural Bangladesh and that microcredit's spillover effects among non-participants reduced poverty among this group by some 1% annually for moderate poverty and 1.3% annually for extreme poverty." While it is difficult to measure all the factors surrounding poverty and the efforts being taken to reduce it, evidence suggests that microfinance and microcredit are strong solutions to addressing poverty, specifically in Bangladesh.

Since its creation, microfinance has been the foundation of combating poverty in Bangladesh. With millions of individuals receiving microloans and other forms of microfinance and many more feeling the trickle-down effect, microcredit is a major influence on economic growth. It has swept through every part of the county and been used by many. If microfinance is a positive solution and not harmful to the poor, one should find decisive evidence located there. Unfortunately for critics, the evidence is almost uniformly positive. The nation has had rapid economic growth, vastly improved its human capital, developed its industry, and made gains in a variety of health and education standards. Additionally, its economic inequality has not worsened to the extent of other Asian countries.

Tazul Islam, in his book *Microcredit and Poverty Alleviation*, closely examined Grameen Bank and its clientele and found some interesting statistics. Although much of the information discussed thus far has shown microfinance in a positive light, Islam (2007) found that microcredit did not directly reach the extreme poor. There are a variety of possible reasons for this. For example, poorer individuals might select themselves out of the program either because they believe they do not qualify, do not have the same entrepreneurial spirit or initiative, or are less likely to assume more risk. Regardless of MFI's rules or credit requirements, Islam (2007) stated that the poorest of the poor may have selected themselves out because they did not believe that they could repay their credit or they simply were not qualified for credit. Furthermore, as discussed previously, part of the reason for a trend toward less impoverished borrowers is the makeup of the loan portfolio. MFIs often compensate for the riskiness and expensive nature of the extreme poor with the less challenging structure of lending to the more moderate poor. This is not an excuse for Grameen Bank and other MFIs, but it might explain this statistic. Nevertheless, it is an issue that MFIs like Grameen Bank (GB) should work to address.

There were additional caveats on the GB microcredit programs and their success. For example, although it is not surprising, the study showed that there was a positive correlation between the size of the loan and the income of the member: the greater income of the borrower, the greater the size of the loan received (Islam 2007). Furthermore, the average income increases were not remarkable for first-time borrowers. However, the number of loans received and the time spent on the program greatly increased the relative benefit of the microloans. If an individual was a member of GB for two years or more, there was a higher chance of a greater increase in income. With that said, it did not result in major growth. To put it in perspective, the "average household income of the fifth-time borrower is 50 percent higher than the first-time borrower" (Islam 2007, 104). Furthermore, the effectiveness of microcredit was, to some extent, dependent upon the starting income of the borrower. The increase in income of GB members was "directly proportional to their starting level of income—the poorer they were to start with, the less the impact of the loan" (Islam 2007, 147). Therefore, while microcredit exhibited positive impacts on the incomes of its borrowers, the results were not even across the board. Additionally, Islam (2007, 156) notes, "The GB's impact on alleviating poverty through changes in the consumption pattern of the rural poor is favorable for the majority of individual clients and households. However, its impact on village level poverty reduction is somewhat smaller." Therefore, while there are a variety of positive outcomes for microcredit borrowers, it is important to keep in mind that poverty reduction at the community level is still small.

While there are some qualifications to the benefits of GB's microcredit program, Islam found many positive outcomes for its members. For instance, the moderate and upper poor and to a smaller extent the extreme poor, who utilized GB's microcredit directly grew their small business incomes (Islam 2007, 103). Despite claims by various critics of microfinance, there was an overall increase in incomes for the average borrower. However, critics often argue that repaying the loan comes at the expense of the poor. While studies might show in increase in income, opponents would say that there is an overall decrease in net worth because the poor must sell their assets to generate income to repay loans (Islam 2007, 110). Therefore, when examining the impact of microfinance, it is critical to also take a look at the overall net worth and capital accumulation of borrowers to measure the overall benefit of the microcredit program. Here are some points that Tazul Islam (2007, 110-111) found:

- More than 50 percent of borrowers did not own cattle before joining the GB although some of them were engaged in raising the cattle of rich farmers on a 50-50 share basis. This figure of 50 percent of borrowers who did not own any cattle was reduced to 33 percent at the time of the survey.

The average number of cattle owned increased by 59 percent during this period.

- Average investment from borrowers' own funds increased from Taka 1,207 for first-time borrowers to Taka 5,128 for members who had borrowed four times and more. The share of equity in total investment increased from 25 percent for the first-time borrowers to nearly 48 percent for members who had borrowed four times or more. This indicates that the more the length of membership with the GB, the more the growth of equity of the borrowers.

- The average amount of working capital per borrower increased nearly three times, from Taka 1217 to Taka 3,607, within about two years. About 65 percent of the households reported accumulation of non-agriculture capital 45 percent of the households reported some investment in crop agriculture after joining the GB.

Despite critics' claims that microfinance forced the poor to sell everything they owned in order to make the weekly (or monthly) payments, the numbers reflect a very different narrative. Islam's results highlight positive outcomes for borrowers. Not only does it appear that borrowers used their credit to make capital improvements instead of personal uses, it also shows that the borrowers were able to purchase assets that improved their lives and businesses. The microloans from GB allowed microentrepreneurs to make investments to grow their businesses, accumulate capital, and improve their quality of life. One additional point: the funding from the credit they received showed particular increases in livestock accumulation. This is important to note because livestock is a very critical tool and resource for the rural poor. Livestock produce milk, meat, eggs, and additional livestock that can be bred and sold. In other words, it is the gift that keeps on giving. It can be used to feed and clothe the family as well as bring in additional income, and it does not require sophisticated training or supplies to maintain or use. These three points further reflect positive outcomes for borrowers and the potential benefits of microfinance.

Asset accumulation was not the only area that saw growth; there were also increases in the standard of living for GB borrowers. When comparing GB members to comparable non-members, there were multiple areas that saw statistically significant improvements relative to their non-GB member counter parts. Islam (2007, 141) noted that:

> The per capita expenditure on food for GB members was 6 percent higher than for non-members of the same groups in project villages, and 15 percent higher than the comparable target-group in control villages. Similarly, the expenditure on clothing for the GB members was 13 percent higher than nonparticipants in project villages and 29 percent higher than the comparable non-members in control villages ... household expenditure in housing by GB members was 32 percent higher of the target groups in project villages and 310 percent higher than the comparable non-members in control villages. Although no significant statistical difference in food expenditure were observed among the GB members, comparable non-members in project and control villages, differences in non-food expenditure among those groups were statistically significant (P<0.000). The differences were mainly for higher housing expenditure of GB members, which indicate their improved standard of living compared to their counterparts.

Not only did borrowers avoid using their assets to repay their loans, they were also able to make important improvements to their quality of living. The income received from their credit allowed them, if not empowered them, to spend more on their homes, purchase more and higher quality food, and buy clothing for their households. These changes reflect an overall life improvement that is part of the process of escaping poverty. These changes mean that individuals and households are climbing out of poverty. Although the process is slow, nevertheless it is happening as a result of microfinance.

Interestingly enough, while examining GB and its results, Islam also found that GB had a positive impact on nonmembers. Not only did members benefit from the credit that they received, but their increased incomes also helped the community around them. The benefits to borrowers did not hurt or negatively impact local nonmembers. Islam (2007, 103) found that in villages that GB operated, nonmember households have incomes which are nearly 11 percent higher than those in comparable households in control villages, which "implies that some proportion of the benefits from the GB have also *trickled out* to local nonmember households." While there is still much debate over the macro effects of microfinance, Islam's research shows that MFIs can impact more than just their membership. Microcredit can help borrowers grow their business and improve their standard of living and also have positive repercussions for the entire community. If microfinance is to have a major impact on macro poverty levels, this has to be the first step.

One might be justified in being skeptical of microfinance deserving of praise if not for studies connecting poverty reduction and microcredit. At its founding, Bangladesh was war-torn and struggled by nearly every economic measurement. It would face several massive natural disasters and foreign aid cuts in the 1990s. Furthermore, unlike many Asian countries, it is not geographically attractive as an international trading partner. However, it continued to grow at rapid rates. Yunus and his Grameen Bank are major factors in poverty reduction in the country. They help millions of individuals and families to the extent of impacting macroeconomic trends. If interest rates were truly harmful to the poor or if microloans were as negative as critics claim, Bangladesh would not be experiencing the level of economic growth that it currently enjoys. The reverse is true: if microfinance is actually a positive force, one would expect to see major improvements on the macro level. Furthermore, studies have been undertaken to examine the relationship between poverty reduction and microfinance in Bangladesh. Shahidur Khandker's study, along with others, represents the positive correlation and causation between microfinance and development gains. No other country experiences microfinance to the extent of Bangladesh. Therefore, it serves as an excellent case study of the macro and micro impact of microlending. The extent that it helps Bangladesh is still a matter of debate but the fact remains that it is a positive force for development and growth.

CHAPTER 7

GREEN MICROFINANCE: THE BEST OF BOTH WORLDS

While a consensus has formed on the need for action concerning pollution and environmental degradation, there is still strong disagreement on the solutions necessary to correct this manmade problem. As countries argue over who is going to pay for fixing it, nongovernmental organizations (NGOs) and private enterprises have proposed many different technologies and programs aimed at creating a greener global economy. One of the difficulties that countries face in resolving environmental problems has to do with the inability of developing countries to find affordable solutions. With their focus on fighting poverty and raising per-capita income, they often view addressing pollution as a lower priority. However, this does not have to be an either-or issue. Microfinance can serve as a powerful tool to target green initiatives and technologies in order to fight poverty, grow less developed economies, and improve third-world nations' environmental impact.

It is understandable that industrialized countries are often held responsible for pollution and global emissions, but studies show that developing countries are exacerbating the problem. For example, "In 2012, developing countries like China, India, and Mexico produced 59 percent of the world's carbon dioxide emissions, while [industrialized] countries and regions like the EU, US, and Russia emitted 41 percent (Roberts 2013)." Due to their rapid rate of growth and production, developing countries have disregarded their pollution levels. At the same time, with the exception of Japan, developed countries have decreased the amount of CO_2 that they produce but this has not been enough to counteract growing emissions in countries such as China (Roberts 2013). To clarify, it is critical that more advanced countries lead by example and make the greatest efforts toward combating pollution and environmental degradation. Developed countries, with their levels of wealth and technology use, are in the best position to immediately tackle many of the environmental problems facing the world today. However, no solution is complete without addressing the growing rates of emissions and ecological harm coming from less-advanced nations.

Unfortunately, due to the nature of being less developed, third-world nations prioritize spending on economic aid to address their high levels of poverty. It is understandable that poorer nations would place such an emphasis on fighting poverty. The World Bank (2016) found that, in 2012, almost 12.7 percent or, in other words, 896 million people lived at or below $1.90 a day. This stunning figure is hard to comprehend and does not fully portray the true levels of poverty that families in developing countries face. However, there does not have to be a choice between protecting the environment and helping the poor. With the right strategy, one can address the deep roots of poverty as well as the growing level of emissions and degradation coming from developing countries.

While overcoming poverty is a major issue, a growing problem for many poor nations is the increased impact of climate change and environmental degradation. Since less-developed countries bear most of the impact of environmental issues, fixing the problem should be a major concern for them as well. Part of the reason they

receive the greatest harm is because of poverty's tendency to use up
the resources that are immediately available instead of investing in
sustainable income-generating practices. For instance, instead of
purchasing a more efficient stove or lighting source, the poor are
likely to use more wood to burn. This means more pollution, more
trees being cut down, and worse living conditions for the family
in the home. Furthermore, poverty has led to rapid population
growth, which is a major challenge faced by many third-world
nations. It causes different negative outcomes, such as pressure on
arable land, an inability to produce enough food, congestion, and
production practices and technologies that tend to be less efficient,
causing more pollution and energy usage (Bowen 1999).

Microloans in and of themselves are "green." By allowing people
to increase their incomes, they generally decrease those individuals'
environmental impact. Whether it is by investing in a more
effective stove instead of using more wood or purchasing a solar
flashlight instead of using more batteries, people use microloans to
make long-term investments that improve their quality of life and
the environment. This point was explained well in the Scientific
American (2009):

> Example after example over the last three decades have proven
> the concept that when poor people are given opportunities
> to earn a living in a legitimate and sustainable fashion, they
> have little or no need to pillage their surrounding natural
> resources to shelter or feed themselves. Also, most of the
> financial institutions involved in microfinance hold up
> sustainability as a precondition for awarding loans. Others
> encourage greener businesses by offering lower interest
> rates to borrowers with sustainability-oriented plans.

Even now, microloans are having a positive impact on the
environment in third-world countries. Whether it is a requirement

to be more sustainable, an incentive with the interest rate, or the general impact that it has on allowing individuals to afford to purchase less harmful products and equipment; microloans are "green" while creating economic development and poverty reduction. MFIs can use a variety of methods and incentives, such as decreased interest rates and specialized microloans for the purchase of environmentally friendly products or improvements to specifically target pollution, biological, and ecological improvement goals. Microfinance, specifically microcredit, can direct its services toward turning the poor into eco-entrepreneurs who are socially and economically productive rather than objects of charity.

> Recent innovations with microloans help them specifically target environmental protection as a second goal, alongside poverty reduction. Dr. Rouf (2012, 87) explains that green microfinance assists microenterprises by helping them invest in capital improvements. In particular, they target marginalized female entrepreneurs in order to empower them in climbing the socio-economic ladder. Furthermore, Dr. Rouf (2012, 87) states that green microcredit programs follow the "mantra of: recycle, refine and reuse resources. Green businesses are not harmful to the environment; rather they accelerate green social development that is people-centered, fosters human health, promotes social justice, generates income, addresses the issue of poverty and reduces waste in the environment. It not only seeks profit, but it also looks at ecological balance within businesses, resources, the environment and society. Green microbusiness can increase marginalized people's income in order to survive, improve their quality of life as well preserve the environment."

Green microloans are designed to achieve the mutually beneficial goals of helping the poor develop income-generating activities while reducing their environmental impact. While many believe that protecting the environment and solving poverty are two different and mutually exclusive goals, microcredit institutions believe that green microloans can achieve both objectives.

While microcredit was invented by Muhammad Yunus in the 1970s, green microcredit is a relatively new innovation. Very few studies have been done to measure their impact on pollution and natural resource degradation reduction. However, institutions around the world have begun to utilize and experiment with the strategy. For instance, "In San Francisco, 230 investors have formed the New Resource Bank with a focus on financing 'green' business and community and sustainable development" (Rouf 2012, 91). The better the understanding the public has of the connection between poverty and environmental issues, the more attention will be directed to finding solutions to both. While countries still disagree over who will pay for the costs of international environmental protection legislation, investors and NGOs have begun to try different options. It is very likely that, over the next few years, more research will examine the impact that microloans have on the environment. Until then, studies show that microloans can be a very effective mechanism for addressing poverty and achieving their targeted goals. By their nature, poverty and the environment are very closely intertwined. The poor are dependent upon the environment, have little to fall back on when there are shortcomings in natural resources or land usage, and are often unable to move or adjust when there are natural disasters. As people better understand that connection, they will pursue solutions that address both sides.

While more research is needed before a conclusion on green microfinance can be reached, the evidence shows that green microcredit has the potential to be a powerful tool in fighting poverty and improving third-world nations' environmental impact. As mentioned earlier, the statistics show that while the developed world shares a major portion of the blame for the level of emissions, no plan will fully correct the problem without including developing countries in the solution. Third-world nations tend to receive the majority of the problems associated with climate change and environmental degradation. However, studies show that improving the ability of the poor to generate income encourages them to reduce their levels of degradation and pollution. Much of the research pertaining to microcredit shows its ability to reduce poverty and increase the incomes of the poor and extreme poor. While this impact in and of itself has positive environment repercussions, microfinance can specifically be used to target green objectives. Institutions can use interest rate incentives, sustainability requirements, and other methods to encourage borrowers to invest in more sustainable practices. By using green microcredit, institutions can help the poorest of the poor provide for their families as well as protect the opportunities of future generations.

CHAPTER 8

WHAT IS HOLDING MICROFINANCE BACK?

While groups and individuals have attempted to study microfinance and its impact on the poor, none have been able to fully evaluate MFIs' progress. Therefore, the significance of their programs remains controversial and debatable. As discussed earlier, most studies on the subject show signs of success and reinforce the belief that MFIs can substantially contribute to combating extreme poverty. Those who examine specific areas with semi-controlled population groups find that microlending and other microfinance services tend to have positive results. Unfortunately, studies do not always examine the whole situation or portray the full picture, and it is critical to clarify the limitations of MFIs.

From the outset, microfinance institutions faced an uphill battle. The nature of the industry means that they tend to be located in hard-to-serve areas with a difficult clientele, often individuals that banks and other companies choose to avoid. The extreme poor in developing countries are often in geographically hard-to-reach areas. They lack effective transportation systems, cellular and Internet communication with the outside world is limited, and various environmental complications regularly impact operations. Furthermore, the specific clientele is hard to serve. The poorest of the poor do not have formal educations and often are limited in their reading and writing capabilities. Explaining the contractual terms of loans and complex financial issues is challenging, if not impossible. This is one reason that many banks avoid serving the extremely poor altogether. These poor entrepreneurs must overcome the same difficulties when growing a business or creating an income: Lack of an education in math, reading, and writing hampers their efforts to manage their finances, find and utilize business opportunities, locate the lowest prices, and sell to customers. Additionally, they have very little experience with credit and financial services. It can be hard for them to fully understand and appreciate the options available to them.

Studies that compare MFI clientele to general populations or control groups might not take into consideration the difficulty of serving such a clientele. If the rural and extreme poor were easy to serve, banks would have long been lending to them. However, MFIs saw opportunity where others did not. They understand the situation and believe that they can offer financial services to the rural poor and still make a profit. When reviewing studies done on the subject or other related economic development issues, it is important to understand and appreciate the challenge in combating poverty. Even if progress is slow, it still has a life-changing impact on the poor.

With that said, not all of the bias around microfinance studies favors the MFIs. The clientele is not randomized and therefore makes for difficult comparisons with the outside population. MFIs do have standards and qualifications for their customers, which can remove individuals who could negatively impact studies. As Armendariz and Morduch (2010, 309) write:

> The challenges in evaluating arise because no microfinance program lends to random citizens. Instead, lenders carefully select areas in which to work and clients to whom to lend. When the characteristics that make borrowers different from nonborrowers are observable, the relevant

conditioning variables (age, education, social status, and so forth) can be accounted for in impact evaluations. Often, though, what makes clients different is not measured— borrowers may, for example, have a more entrepreneurial spirit, enjoy better business connections, or may be more focused than nonparticipants.

Any of these features would make borrowers more likely to succeed and climb out of poverty relative to their neighbors. Because of their willingness to take credit for their businesses, they are more likely to be risk-takers, be innovative, and have a better understanding of credit and finances, all of which would put them at an advantage, regardless of the influence of microlending. With this understanding, it seems likely that the clients of microlending would be more likely to improve than those without microcredit simply because of their background or personality, which limits the ability to effectively measure the impact of MFIs. As a matter of fact, one study on the subject reinforced this conclusion and found that microcredit had a better outcome on borrowers who lived above the poverty mark when compared to those below it (Karnani 2007). The argument was that those below the poverty line were less likely to take risk and therefore would not increase their revenues to the same degree as those with higher incomes. Comparatively, those who lived above the poverty line were already more likely to take risk and invest in technology to improve their microbusinesses, thereby increasing their profits.

Furthermore, the simple fact that microfinance institutions can show positive results does not prove that they are making worthwhile investments. As discussed earlier, when measuring the impact of tools that combat poverty, it is important to consider the cost-effectiveness of a program. Therefore, when contemplating microfinance, one must consider whether it is a better use of money than other forms of development aid. Even if all studies showed

MFIs to decrease poverty, if they were not as successful as other types of development programs, then investments and donations should be diverted elsewhere.

Unfortunately, MFIs are often unable to achieve their full potential because of factors that impede their growth. Aside from geographic and client-related issues, many challenges prevent them from expanding and improving their efforts. For instance, most development programs have close relationships with their local and national governments. Either for political purposes or out of genuine appreciation of their efforts, governments often encourage and assist nonprofits and foreign aid. The same cannot be said for MFIs. In developing countries, there has been little action or assistance from governments (Morduch 2009). Governments and their agencies are very apprehensive about microcredit. However, this feeling is mutual. Many MFIs see government as intrusive or harmful to their operations, even if elected officials and government agencies have good intentions.

Lack of Support From the Government

Governments in some developing countries have tried to assist MFIs, and others have opposed their operations, both with negative consequences. Sometimes, the unintended consequences of government actions can be extremely problematic for microlenders. In some low-income countries, governments have forgiven the loans made to the poor by their state banks. Mistakenly believing that these actions also forgave the loans of private MFIs, debtors refused to repay their microloans or allowed them to go into default (Ledgerwood 1999). Such government actions cause confusion among the poor, with devastating effects on MFIs.

Unfortunately, many governments do not appreciate or value the work done by MFIs. Sometimes believing that they prey upon the poor, governments look down on microfinance institutions and refuse to assist or protect them. One example is India, where "Some state governments' attitudes toward MFIs ranged from apathy to hostility" (Srinivasan 2010, 5). This can cause problems when there is conflict or danger to MFIs. In 2009, in the Kolar district of India, there was a mass default on microloans, causing MFIs to lose millions. Due to complaints about the MFIs' quality of customer service and other factors, religious and community leaders convinced otherwise responsible borrowers to join the protest and default on their loans. Srinivasan (2010, 5), in *Microfinance India State of the Sector Report*, states, "The apathy of the state government is palpable in letting a problem of this magnitude fester for more than 18 months. There had been a clear violation of law in inciting people to renege on a validly executed loan contract, using religion as the trigger. MFIs have stopped lending in Kolar and similar other locations. ... The religious leadership has to rethink its position: whether it causes more misery and less benefit to its flock in issuing such edicts in a facile and unthinking manner." Such actions by communities have long-term and short-term effects on microfinance institutions and their operations. As a result, they often reduce services to an entire area and similar locations, to prevent further losses. This harms the prospects of poor individuals who desired to obtain microloans or needed credit to improve their situations. It does not only hurt those who participated in the protests but also those who were law-abiding and innocent.

Actions such as mass defaults and conflicts scare off MFIs that are attempting to provide services to the very poor. Their borrowers already have weak credit histories and struggle to obtain loans from reputable sources. Situations like these reduce their chances to obtain a loan. Many of these events could be stopped or ended sooner if governments upheld contracts and protected MFIs. Simply upholding loan agreements would provide much-needed security and stability for MFIs and allow them to continue to run their operations. But when governments turn a blind eye or support the protestors, MFIs lose faith in the system and choose to provide services elsewhere. This hurts the poor that they intend to help and limits economic development. In many cases, MFIs are not seeking special treatment; they merely want fair and stable rule of law.

Government Regulation

Government opposition to microfinance often goes beyond merely turning a blind eye to the problems that MFIs face. In many cases, regulations put in place harm their ability to assist the poor. Since the 1970s, many developing countries have attempted to deregulate and promote a more laissez-faire economic system. This "liberalization," in the area of financial markets in particular, has helped economic growth and the creation of wealth (Kloppenburg 2006, 2). Due to deregulation and an antiquated legal system, most developing countries have no regulations in place to monitor and manage MFIs. Many MFIs continue to exit in the informal sector, where the legal system is unclear concerning their operations. In many cases, they do so with the full knowledge and awareness of their governments (Ledgerwood 1999). This lack of direction and definition impedes the ability of MFIs to operate and makes the legal environment unstable. Just like many of their customers, MFIs must work in the informal sector, not knowing what is legal and what crosses the line. With a change in leadership, loss of favor by elected officials, or a shift in government, the operations of MFIs could be vastly impacted in the blink of an eye. This instability hurts their ability to plan, grow, and fully serve the poor. If governments want the poor to have access to financial services that enable them to save, invest, and develop, then they must establish clear legal frameworks for microbusinesses as well as MFIs. Once that has taken place, they must enforce their laws so that MFIs know how and where they can operate and be protected by a fair and just legal system.

Furthermore, the regulation systems in place in many developing countries limits the number and quality of services provided by MFIs. In various low-income countries, such as India, the legal system prevents MFIs from providing some services, such as savings accounts, for the very poor (Srinivasan 2010; Churchill and Frankiewicz 2006). This is because "Regulatory policies in most countries prevent nonprofit, unregulated organizations from collecting savings, because there is no way to insure deposits placed at an unregulated institution" (White and Campion 2002, 26). Thus even simple services are impeded by harmful regulations. Antiquated laws and an unclear legal system can also block insurance, lending, housing, and other services that could otherwise be provided to the extreme poor. Although many of these laws have the best intentions, they have a price. Most often, that price is at the expense of the poorest of the poor. The wealthy can find ways around laws or encourage governments to change policies or create exceptions. The poor do not have these options. They are unable to defend themselves or fully research laws, and they struggle to change public policy. When governments pass policies to regulate MFIs or financial institutions, very often it results in fewer options for the poor. Unfortunately, bad regulations are not the only hurdle that MFIs face. As described by Yunus (2007, 7), "Even an excellent government regulatory regime for business is not enough to ensure that serious social problems will be confronted, much less solved." Improving the legal system for MFIs and the informal sector is only a piece in the puzzle, albeit a major one.

Government Assistance Can Hurt

Although government opposition and regulation can hurt the MFIs' cause, government help can be just as burdensome. In an attempt to reduce interest rates from microfinance institutions and provide assistance, some developing countries offer or mandate subsidies for MFIs. The logic is that MFIs must charge high prices (also known as interest rates) on their microloans in order to remain profitable and stay in business. If the government provides subsides to MFIs, they can charge less on their microcredit, and loans can be more affordable for the poor. The intention is positive but misinformed. Although the practice of offering subsidies is common in developing countries, the results can be counterproductive (Goldberg and Palladini 2010, 45). Subsidies can be extremely harmful, and can jeopardize the outreach of MFIs altogether.

The first problem of public subsidies, particularly those aimed at MFIs, is that they often come with strings attached. As wolves dressed in sheep's clothing, they appear helpful on the outside but come with dangerous red tape and bureaucracy. As described by Goldberg and Palladini (2010, 81), "For example, governments unnecessarily limit the market by requiring a subsidiary specialized in leasing. The lack of clear definition for leasing and the responsibilities and rights of each party in a leasing contract also limit the market's expansion." Strange rules are often attached to funding that limit the practices of firms that do not qualify for subsidies. Because not every MFI qualifies for subsidies, governments limit funding to a few select organizations; those that do not receive funding can be legally barred from offering certain services. Those that are able to obtain funding can find that it opens the door to increased government review, auditing, and regulation. Claiming to they ensure that MFIs are spending their money properly, government agencies can become burdensome in overseeing the practices of MFIs. When the government provides funding, it inadvertently becomes a part owner of the business and views itself as such. Sadly, receiving funding is not always a choice. It sometimes is mandated.

To make matters worse, when subsidies are introduced into the microfinance sector, it drives out competition. Although there may appear to be choices in the beginning, subsidies quickly create an unfair advantage and serve as an unofficial mandate: if you do not have the subsidy, you may go out of business. The nature of subsidies is that they tend to go to a few well-developed organizations or companies. Governments rarely make large expenditures to subsidize the operations of small start-up MFIs. Larger, more developed companies tend to be more likely to obtain subsidies. They are better organized to compete for them, more established, and better known, and they can make a more effective case for why they are uniquely qualified to obtain government funding. This practice ensures that there are winners and losers among MFIs. MFIs that do not receiving funding struggle to lower interest rates to compete with the subsidized firms. This narrows the field down to fewer, larger organizations providing services to the poor.

Some of the most attractive features of microfinance fade away when subsidies occur. Because they decrease the number of MFIs, the ones remaining become bigger and less flexible. By nature, microfinance institutions are agile, adaptive, and cost-efficient. Because of the nature of their industry, they must be able to operate within small profit margins. They must adapt to the culture, geography, and demographics of their clientele. Additionally, the sector is growing and strong when MFIs are numerous and able to reach out to various geographic areas. If subsidies pick winners and losers, the few that remain are unable to serve the wide range of geographic areas. Furthermore, the process hurts the poor that governments are attempting to assist. MFIs provide selection and focus on providing quality service to the poor, a group that was once ignored in this area. However, subsidies reduce the number of MFIs and reduce the competition between them. This provides the poor with fewer choices in financial services and makes the institutions that lend to them bigger and bulkier, reducing the flexibility and helpful practices that made them unique.

A centerpiece of microfinance has been the free-market nature of the industry. They appear to take a laissez-faire economic approach to combating poverty. Subsidies remove the free-market benefits. MFIs are capitalistic organizations and social businesses attempting to make a profit by solving a world problem and helping people; it's a win-win. When subsidies are introduced, they force MFIs to cease competing for the customer, instead competing for funding. Originally, the most important issue for MFIs was serving their clients. MFIs need to provide quality customer service, affordable interest rates, and flexible repayment plans, along with services that might complement their business model and be cost effective. However, certain standards and goals need to be met to obtain government funding. Once it is introduced, MFIs must focus upon meeting government criteria instead of zeroing in on the individuals they intend to aid.

Lastly, dependence on government funding and large donors harms the long-term success of MFIs. Subsidies and strong donor networks can become crutches for MFIs and prevent them from remaining independent or flexible. The often-optimistic dream for MFIs is that they can become financially independent. However, in some cases this may be impractical. Instead, the goal should be to reduce dependence upon exterior funding as much as possible. By becoming financially solvent and self-funding through the profits of their operations, they become less susceptible to the dangers of losing a donation or government contract. If there is global recession or exterior events outside of the control of the MFI, funding can end suddenly. Governments can change laws, and funding priorities of donors in Western countries can change. Although many MFIs are nonprofits and have effectively relied upon donations, this is discouraged. The nature of their operations and small profit margins might mean that some MFIs are always dependent upon some funding. It is critical that MFIs use funding only to grow their operations and that they not become dependent upon one or a few major sources. Furthermore, one of the dangers of relying upon donations or subsidies is that the focus tends to shift to obtaining additional funding and away from providing financial services. To increase funding and help operations, MFIs devote more resources to fundraising activities, instead of providing services to the poor that they intend to help. The focus of MFIs must always be upon providing quality and affordable service.

Government Intervention

Since the spread of microlending, governments have attempted to join the cause and deliver microfinance services to the poor themselves. Viewing it as an alternative to other forms of aid, both domestic and international government institutions have tried providing microcredit and other microfinance products to the poor. Unfortunately, besides being ineffective themselves, their participation often has unforeseen consequences on private sector MFIs. When governments try to deliver these services to the poor, they very often cannot provide the same standard and level of quality as traditional MFIs. This is because "Government institutions may lack the incentives to monitor such loans effectively or control administrative costs, because success is often defined in terms of credit disbursements rather than loan portfolio quality or operational efficiency" (Goldberg and Palladini 2010, 45). Many developing countries do not have the time and resources to ensure the necessary steps and procedures that increase loan repayment and verify the integrity of the borrower. Furthermore, government institutions do not have the same incentives as other MFIs. Private-sector MFIs are dedicated to obtaining high repayment rates, becoming self-sustaining, and weaning borrowers off the programs. The mindset of government institutions is entirely different. Their budgets are often dependent upon the number of individuals in the program, which is an incentive to increase the number of borrowers. Less attention is paid to the credit of borrowers, their likelihood of repayment, or their use of funds. Sometimes this is intentional—to increase their funding—and sometimes it is the result of carelessness from programs that are too bloated, disorganized, and ineffective.

These poorly managed and dysfunctional programs can cause a massive financial drain on governments. This happens when borrowers start to look at government microloans as handouts that do not require repayment. When governments follow the same guidelines as MFIs by not requiring collateral (which is a commonplace tactic used my MFIs), borrowers assume they are similar to any other social program and do not need to be repaid. This lower repayment rate further weakens the success of government microfinance and hurts government institution's ability to focus and fund other programs.

Unfortunately, the problems of government microfinance often impact surrounding MFIs. While they might have been sustainable and effective originally, with the introduction of government microfinance, MFIs began to suffer from the same hurdles that government institutions face. Borrowers often are unable to understand the difference between the various microfinance providers. When repayment rates decrease for government providers, private-sector MFIs can experience the same effect (Ledgerwood 1999). This confusion impacts the ability of MFIs to reach their necessary repayment rates, hurting their sustainability. Furthermore, the government institutions are funded by domestic and foreign governments. Therefore, they do not require full repayment and can charge lower interest rates. This makes other MFIs uncompetitive. Private-sector MFIs have to charge interest rates high enough to sustain their practices and maintain certain standards of quality within their portfolios. Governments can charge lower rates and take the risky clients that can hurt the returns for nonprofit and for-profit MFIs. This burden has the potential to run them out of business. While governments often provide a lower quality of service and are less self-sufficient, their operations have negative consequences for surrounding MFIs.

Lack of Infrastructure

One of the largest hurdles MFIs face in making a major impact on poverty is actually not financial; it is overcoming the startling lack of infrastructure many poor communities face. The poor are largely rural and in small villages around the world. This makes it more burdensome for microbusiness owners to expand their markets or bring in goods and services. Many rural communities lack effective transportation to other areas. The roads might be unusable except by foot traffic, and villages often lack running or clean water or unpredictable or no electricity. MFIs can only work with the tools that they are given. If a community has no access to outside markets to bring in or export supplies and lacks basic health care and clean and affordable water and energy, the poor will always struggle to escape poverty. Creating and expanding businesses requires open markets and people able to purchase goods and services. While wealth can start and evolve from these small, rural villages, it takes time and multiple loans. With a lack of usable roads and transportation systems, the poor are unable to sell their goods and services to a wider market that might pay more. They are also unable to import resources that they might need or bring in newer technology to upgrade their operations. They often have to combat civil conflict, public health issues, the struggle to obtain clean water and food, and they most likely do not have cheap and consistent access to electricity. These challenges make starting and growing small businesses harder more time-consuming and limits options for growth. Although microfinance undoubtedly plays an important role in combating poverty, developing and improving basic infrastructure in third-world countries is imperative to combating poverty as a whole.

Lack of a Quality Educational System

The fundamental lack of quality educational systems in third-world countries has a detrimental impact on the potential of microentrepreneurs. Not only do weak educational institutions negatively affect the poor in terms of developing skills that will lead to employment, it also hurts the ability of small business owners to start, grow, and expand their productions. For the same reasons that a poor educational system can prevent individuals from escaping poverty, lack of education prevents microfinance borrowers from using their microcredit to its full potential. There are almost an unlimited number of explanations for this but we shall examine a few key reasons.

For one thing, a basic education teaches skills that can enable entrepreneurs to grow beyond subsistence. Lessons in math, reading and writing, biology, health, and so on, can provide knowledge that leads to better decisions, more efficient practices, and higher standards of living. Without the ability to read and write and do simple algebra, a person's world is limited. Those skills in particular enable and empower people to take advantage of more opportunities. For example, being able to read, write, and do math can allow individuals to secure more sophisticated loans, make decisions on which financial or consumer products are the best for them, know what prices to charge for their services to achieve the best rate of return, etc.

Furthermore, education allows entrepreneurs to gather information that will impact their businesses. For example, Mannan, in his book *Growth and Development of Small Enterprise: The Case of Bangladesh* (90), notes, "The village potters, for example, have been found to be largely unaware of the large variety of novelty and product differentiation that could be produced from clay having high demand in the urban areas. Such a situation arises due to non-existence of organized programs for dissemination of market information to producers." Whether by making unique products, being able export products to urban areas with higher demand, having the ability to learn of different and more affordable options to purchase material, or reading a newspaper to find out how current events might have an impact, basic skills would enable microentrepreneurs to achieve more.

Many microentrepreneurs struggle with high competition and limited markets. As previously mentioned, the poor are often in underdeveloped areas without an effective transportation system to move products. This limits their markets. To make matters worse, multiple microentrepreneurs often sell similar products in the same location. For instance, many operate out of public markets. This leads to a cluster of vendors selling identical goods and services right next to each other. This lack of variation restricts their ability to make more than marginal profits (Webster and Fidler 1996). Part of the reason for this is the lack of a standard education. Many underdeveloped nations have apprenticeship programs, but they do not go beyond developing basic skills. Webster and Fidler (1996, 14) explain, "Because most apprenticeship training simply passes on known practices, the skills of its graduates tend to be based on emulation rather than innovation, a sure recipe for noncompetitive production." This flaw in the education tradition hinders innovation and growth. While countries like the United States, Europe, and BRIC countries have focused upon innovation and technological sophistication as key to future economic growth, developing countries have struggled to move their educational systems in that direction. This detail holds them back and will prevent them from catching up to the rest of the world.

Despite the problematic educational systems in countries they serve, MFIs can and have found ways to adjust. Many microfinance institutions include training in their programs to help microentrepreneurs learn skills and grow their businesses. By giving advice, teaching lessons, and having microentrepreneurs meet together, MFIs spread communication and core business skills among the borrowers. Many of these programs are still new, but they will continue to grow and become instrumental to the process of microlending. While the entrepreneurs benefit by learning, the MFIs also gain from the success of the microbusinesses. When microentrepreneurs succeed, they are more likely to repay their loans and require additional credit to continue expanding.

Property Rights

Along with an education, basic infrastructure, and so on, property rights—or the lack thereof—serve as one of the greatest hindrances to economic development in high poverty areas. As discussed previously, property rights are a cornerstone of any business. There is a strong need for microentrepreneurs to feel that they are safe and that they truly have ownership of their belongings. Unfortunately, that is not the case in many developing countries. Along with geopolitical instability, weather and environmental changes, and economic factors, without clear property ownership, they are left in uncertainty. Small business in third-world countries are often quasi-legal or in a gray area concerning their legal status. With poor regulation and heavy government planning, the poor are unable to get official approval for their businesses and have to operate in the dark. The term "illegal business" is often associated with drug trafficking, human trafficking, street gangs, and other malicious activity. Unfortunately, that is not generally the case. Many illegal businesses in third-world countries have perfectly noble operations; they might be food carts, brick and pottery makers, sellers of firewood, etc. These services and products are critical to the surrounding community, but because of the inefficiencies of government, their owners cannot get approval. Part of the inefficiency is the lack of guidance in establishing property rights. The example commonly cited is Peru, but the problem persists around the globe. Many of the poor build homes and businesses on unused land and assume land ownership simply because they were there first; this is also known as squatters rights. This means that millions, perhaps billions, of people in the world have no clear and legal ownership of their property. This prevents them from using their land as collateral to receive a loan, establishing legitimate business operations, having a sense of stability, and making large, long-term investments in their property.

Microloans can be extremely helpful in starting and growing microbusiness. However, they are limited in their potential when there is no clear legal ownership of a property. Murky ownership makes the microloan a riskier investment. In addition, the borrower's business can only grow so big without clear legal ownership. These businesses could be shut down by the government at any time and can only receive so much capital from lenders. Moreover, small and micro-sized businesses are dependent upon collaboration. They need to form agreements with suppliers and purchasers, write contracts, and so on. Without property rights or government enforcement of contracts, microentrepreneurs face high transaction costs, lower profit margins, and less stability in an environment that is already in constant flux.

Inflation

The silent killer of savings and one of the most underestimated dangers to the poor, inflation can have a devastating impact. Overnight, savings accounts can be wiped out. All the hard work that the poor undertake to save small amounts for future purchases (an unnatural process in underdeveloped areas) is washed away by higher prices for goods. This happens with the government spends more money than it has, leading to more money circulating in the system. At first, this may seem ideal; more money in the system means that people have more money to buy things, which might benefit the very poor. Unfortunately, when everyone has more money, the money becomes less valuable. As the government borrows more money from investors and prints more cash, the value of the currency becomes lower and lower. This is why items at the grocery store cost more than they did years ago. The items have not changed; the value of the dollar that buys them has changed.

As the government borrows and spends more money, investors become less trusting and charge a higher interest rate on government bonds. Just as an MFI would charge higher interest rates to a risky customer, when governments perform risky behavior with their finances they get charged higher rates of interest. This deepens the downward spiral, forcing governments to pay more for borrowing. Often, the only method of paying for those higher interest rates is by printing more money. The end result is a deterioration of the value of the money. Consumers notice that the price of goods, like milk and bread, goes up, along with everything else. A loaf of bread that cost a single dollar now costs three dollars; next year, it will be five dollars, and in a couple years—ten dollars, and so on. Countries like Zimbabwe show just how dangerous inflation can be. Eventually, if unabated, inflation grows exponentially. In some cases, businesses have to pay their workers two or three times each day because the wage is constantly increasing. Employees want to ensure that they get paid, and businesses cannot afford to pay them all at one time. Inflation can become so volatile that prices change every day and salaries can change by the end of the workday.

What sometimes happens is something I noticed while visiting Argentina. Although she was born and raised in Argentina, my friend saved her money in the form of US dollars. When she wanted to buy something, she would find a local business that would exchange her dollars for pesos. Furthermore, when I entered a business or walked down a street, individuals would notice that I was an American and ask if I wanted to sell my US dollars to them. Although this entire practice was extralegal, we never had to worry about finding someone that would exchange our dollars so that we could purchase something. People who lived in Argentina could not rely on pesos to retain their value, so they resorted to a more stable currency: the US dollar. Furthermore, by the time I left, the US dollar had increased in value compared to the peso, so it seemed that everything was cheaper for me. On the other side of the equation, everyone with pesos found items more expensive. The business owners found the value of their goods changing every day, and there was nothing that they could do to prevent it.

As one can imagine, this is a very destructive problem for businesses. It means that they cannot save or invest; their savings are devalued constantly. It becomes harder to know what to charge for products and services. With that said, not everything is worse. When inflation is rampant, businesses can expect higher and higher payments for goods. As a result, loans become cheaper, relatively speaking. If your loan charges 10 percent interest but inflation is 8 percent, your actual interest rate is 2 percent. This is because, with all else equal, higher inflation means customers pay more for their goods and services. While costs have also gone up by the same amount, their loan interest rates have plateaued. This makes it easier to pay back loans. As Srinivasan (2010, 76-77) writes, "Financial savings are suitable in economics that have stable conditions. When inflation rates creep up, savings in financial assets end up as a tax on the poor. There have been countries with [hyper-inflation] where the value of savings would have been very little over time. The case of Zimbabwe and Mexico where inflation reached very high levels show that in such situations, the poor would have been better off to borrow and invest in assets." Lending becomes more affordable. Dollar for dollar, it can even be profitable to buy hard assets, like precious metals, tools, livestock, and so on, hold them, and then sell them. With inflation, the monetary price of those goods is ever-increasing while the currency is constantly losing its value.

For the same reason, inflation is cruel to MFIs. MFIs make their profits from small-margin microloans. When inflation is a factor, MFIs need to charge much higher rates of interest to compensate for their lost relative income. MFIs profit little off each individual loan; they need many microloans to sustain operations. Inflation eats away at these margins, cutting profits for the lender. Therefore, inflation not only destroys the savings of the poor, it can bankrupt microlenders as well. It stalls the efforts of all of those attempting to combat poverty. If governments of developing countries want to address poverty and promote economic growth, they must first limit monetary inflation. Without maintaining fiscal control, poverty can never be fully solved.

Macroeconomic and Political Trends

Above all, microfinance is only as effective as its surroundings. If an area's culture, regulatory system, and economic trends are hostile to MFIs, their impact is limited. When it comes to the various macroeconomic movements that can negatively impact MFIs, one key factor is the stability of the participant country's political climate. White and Campion (2002, 30-31) write:

A country's overall political stability can significantly influence a transforming MFI's ability to attract and maintain access to investment capital. Political instability can lead to arbitrary changes in monetary policy, such as statutory reserve requirements, foreign-exchange holding policies, or directed lending mandates. Unstable political environments may also magnify competing political agendas among government officials, including bank regulators, creating significant delays in license processing.

Despite efficient business practices, high demand for microloans and other positive features that are in their realm of control, MFIs suffer from political instability. Financial institutions require stability and consistency and are adverse to risk, due to the already risky nature of their industry. Instead of spending limited capital, time, and energy, trying to win the favor of the political party in control, MFIs are more likely to simply pursue operations elsewhere, leaving the poor without affordable financial options.

Commonly mistaken for stereotypical big banks, MFIs often become the enemies of ruling governments or competing political interests. Worse yet, as discussed previously, MFIs are often discouraged and shut down, due to their high rates of interests. Even the threat of this possibility scares MFIs and their customers. When customers believe that they might lose their savings or access to credit, they are immediately scared away. The margins for MFIs are small to start with, so any significant loses can be crippling.

Along with political instability, simple macroeconomic trends can hurt the efforts of microfinance institutions. Like any organization dedicated to fighting poverty, MFIs are sensitive to economic trends. Global recessions and price swings can often have a very strong effect on the poorest of the poor. Increases (or decreases) in the price of fuel or food often hurts the poor more than any other group of people. Therefore, while microfinance might provide additional options that assist the poor in improving their economic standing, they cannot make up for large global trends. Global recessions can eliminate demand for microentrepreneurs' products, and price increases can reduce their ability to save or invest. Additionally, price swings and recessions can hurt their ability to repay loans. Sudden loss of demand for their goods and services or price increases can make repaying loans impossible. This not only negatively impacts the finances of the MFIs, it can also have long-term repercussions on the poor. The inability to repay a microloan will be a part of their credit history and can limit their future financial options.

Achieving Economies of Scale

Lastly, efficient operations are one of the most critical issues that MFIs face. While many of the major challenges listed are outside of their control, this is one that they have the ability to influence. Microfinance institutions, which work in difficult, poor, and rural areas, struggle to increase profit margins and expand outreach. However, the more they can decrease costs, achieve economies of scale, and establish efficient business practices, the easier it is for them to increase revenue, expand outreach, and help more families. When discussing the difficulties of MFIs, Pagura (2008, 11) gives an excellent explanation of this point:

> In addressing these challenges, some financial organizations take advantage of their proximity to rural clients, but typically they offer only a narrow range of services. In part, this is explained by their unregulated nature, which prevents them from engaging in deposit mobilization and other functions reserved for regulated entities. In part, it is explained by their inability to generate sufficient economics of scale, economies of scope, and portfolio diversification

to lower operating costs and risks. The ability to increase rural outreach in a competitive environment is grounded on declining costs.

Regulation and government intervention can limit the efficiency of MFIs. Controls that define what services MFIs can provide, how services are provided, and that set quotas, rate caps, and so on, can cripple or prevent MFIs from providing assistance to the poor. However, the majority of this burden depends upon the MFIs themselves. It is up to them to find the right balance for number of clients, services to provide, the geographic distance to cover, etc.

This problem will decrease over time as the industry becomes more experienced and better adjusted to its environment. For the most part, MFIs are still new and freshly established. They are still exploring the limitations of their services, testing goals and expectations, and exploring how to provide service. Over time, this will be understood and industry practices will evolve. Until then, there will be a learning curve. Unfortunately, this learning process comes with pains. Combined with the other challenges facing MFIs, the prospects can seem daunting. However, with great care, attention to detail, experimentation, and practice, this can be overcome. One method of achieving economies of scale and reducing costs has been to provide additional services, when legal. Not only does this strategy make MFIs more efficient and productive, it is also common sense that additional services are needed in order to substantially reduce global poverty (Islam 2007). To decrease costs, providing additional services can be an excellent and cost-effective solution. With that said, "mission creep" is a very possible risk for MFIs as financial incentives grow (Brody, Copestake, and Greeley 2005, 1). As MFIs grow and become better adjusted, it is imperative that they do not grow too quickly or attempt to offset costs by providing too many services.

One issue impeding MFIs from improving their practices has

been the lack of capital available. Due to the global recession, MFIs have found it difficult to obtain significant funding from investors and donors. This has limited their growth and potential to serve new areas. While hundreds of millions of individuals could qualify for microfinance, most do not have access. This problem will continue until MFIs can expand. Without access to substantially more capital, MFIs will be unable to achieve the economies of scale necessary to assist that quantity of people. Furthermore, MFIs may desire to provide lending outside of the typical short-term microloans. Unfortunately, the lack of long-term access to consistent funding prevents MFIs from providing loans with longer terms (Churchill and Frankiewicz 2006). Therefore, while these alternative types of loans may be very beneficial to borrowers seeking larger amounts and lower interest rates, they are unobtainable. These types of loans have great potential to assist the poor but, unless MFIs can secure enough long-term, reliable funding, they will not exist. Therefore, as MFIs seeks to expand, grow, develop, improve, and provide additional services, it will take time and additional capital.

Microfinance is and can be effective in reducing poverty. However, it must first overcome the challenges it faces in order to unleash its full potential. *An Analysis of Microfinance and Poverty Reduction in Bayelsa State of Nigeria* provides an excellent summary of the potential of microfinance:

> After a theoretical and empirical exploration of relevant literatures, the paper found that there is a significant relationship between microfinance and poverty reduction; significant difference between microfinance and traditional savings rotating system; loan repayment and poverty reduction; and microfinance and status of women in the society. On the premises of the revelations from this study, we conclude that thus microfinance alone cannot reduce the level of poverty in any given society except the government

provide the basic infrastructural facilities such as good road, constant power supply, good transport system, etc. that is when microfinance will play an effective and efficient role of poverty reduction instrument in contemporary society (Appah, Sophia, and Wisdom 2012, 53).

It would be foolish to view microfinance as a silver bullet or a be-all and end-all solution to poverty reduction. Rather, it should be considered as a major tool in combating extreme poverty. The evidence and research on the subject reinforces the narrative that microfinance can be highly effective when paired with efforts like infrastructure development, healthcare, education, and so on. On its own, it is still helpful and has shown signs of reducing poverty but without assistance overcoming its challenges, microfinance will be slow to achieve this goal.

When examining the subject of poverty and discovering new methods of addressing it, it is important to have the correct perspective. Ringmar (2006, 9) states that the cause of poverty:

Lay not with the poor, the social environments within which they live, nor the capitalistic system, rather, they were attributed to the failure of development theorists and practitioners to reach the poor, understand their environments, and to recognize their potential to be active participants in the economy. In this regard, microcredit is a promising policy, provided it is institutionalized in a poor-friendly manner.

Perhaps the greatest benefit of Yunus's creation of microfinance was the fundamental belief that the poor could be participants and assets to society instead of being viewed as drains on the system. Microentrepreneurs have amazing potential, and microfinance seeks to unlock it. Many development theories rely on the principle that the poor are helpless and seek a savior to rescue them, but this is a false and dangerous paradigm. Instead, they are human beings that have the ability to turn their small shops or stalls into businesses that can employ others and support a family. Rather than believing that the poor cannot save, borrow money, make smart investment decisions, and run a business, development theorists and policymakers should be seeking methods of supporting the initiative and endeavors of poor entrepreneurs. By removing burdensome regulations, limiting and simplifying taxes, allowing nonprofits and MFIs to operate with greater freedom, and focusing their resources on improving rural and underdeveloped communities, governments can have a greater impact on poverty.

CHAPTER 9

THE FUTURE OF MICROFINANCE

Maturing of the Industry

Although the microfinance industry faces many diverse and difficult challenges, it has shown itself to be resilient and adaptive. Despite its trials, microfinance has continued to improve in how it addresses the needs of its clientele. This is partially due to its nature of being a fairly fresh concept. MFIs, such as Grameen Bank, have been around since the 1970s, which means it has not had much time to experiment and grow. Microfinance is becoming more successful as time passes and the industry matures. As MFIs learn how to deal with governments, discover more about processing transactions and delivering services to the poor, and develop "industry norms," they will develop procedures and solutions to problems. Like any simple activity, practice makes perfect; the more practice that MFIs have, the better their service will be to the poorest of the poor.

Innovations

One of the major outcomes of the maturing industry has been innovation in the strategies and practices of MFIs. Not only are MFIs experimenting with various types of services, geographic locations, and technology, they are also examining new methods of delivering services. For example, in order to receive loan payments more conveniently, Banco do Nordeste in Brazil set up an agreement to accept loan payments in various post offices (Drake and Christen 2002). Experiments like that allow MFIs to stay proactive and conform to the needs of the poor. As previously discussed, delivering financial services to the poor can be challenging. Because of this, a large segment of the world's population has been unable to access common financial services and receive credit. In order to address this diverse and growing part of the global population, new strategies and technologies are necessary. Setting up joint operations or agreements with post offices and other governmental and nongovernmental organizations will be critical to the long-term viability of microfinance.

Grameen Bank, with its subsidiaries, has led the way when it comes to innovation and experimentation. One technique it has tried is to create "tension-free" microlending (Armendariz and Murdoch 2010). This approach gives employees of Grameen II flexibility in assisting borrowers in times of need. For instance, if other options do not work, staff of Grameen II can adjust repayment schedules in ways that help the poor. Although this is a risky strategy, it allows borrowers to repay their loans, without damaging their credit history; thus they will still be able to receive credit in the future. Extreme situations can happen. Weather phenomena, crime, health, and other issues can prevent a borrower from being able to repay a loan or miss a single payment. By showing grace and a willingness to adjust payment schedules, the poor are given another chance.

Some of the innovations made with microfinance are more adventurous than others. The organization *CultureBank* provides microfinance to the poor with a slightly different goal. While aiming to reduce poverty, the organization also has the intention of preserving local African culture. In *Microfinance: Perils and Prospects*, Deubel (136-141) explains this strategy:

> By applying a microcredit model, the *CultureBank* provides capital for participants to invest in small enterprises, promotes the conservation of Dogon cultural heritage and increases social capital by fostering contact between participants and joint involvement in income-generating activities. ... In exchange for each object placed in the museum, participants gain eligibility for a small business loan over a four to six month period at 3 percent interest per month. The amount of the loan is determined by the verifiable historical value of the piece that is assessed by the loan manager according to a questionnaire formula. Upon timely repayment, borrowers may opt to renew their loan for an equal or greater amount, thereby gaining access to a steady stream of additional income. This system enables participants to access increasingly large business loans over time in contrast with the finite, short-term profits gained by selling objects. Individuals retain of their objects throughout the process. In the case of loan default, objects remain in the museum's permanent collection but cannot be sold or exchanged at any time. From 1997 to 2002, the bank made 451 total loans (average size US$22) with objects as collateral to 70 borrowers (60 percent women) at 3 percent interest per month. The rate of reimbursement has averaged 94 percent over the life of the project, and women consistently reimburse at a higher rate than men (97 percent compared to 90 percent).

Organizations outside of the typical realm of MFIs have begun to use microcredit as a method of achieving goals aside from reducing poverty. Whether their intentions are to combat environment degradation, global warming, loss of historic culture, or other nontraditional proposals, microfinance has become a tool to address various needs. This strategy is an innovative use of microloans and further displays adaptability and potential of microfinance. Institutions like *CultureBank* continue to make bold attempts at achieving real change. Other organizations have tried to improve their quality of service by "including group loans with social guarantees" (Churchill and Frankiewicz 2006, 21). As more organizations get proactive and the industry continues to mature and evolve, and as more individuals have access to microfinancial services, it will be amazing to see what happens.

Technological Advances

On the forefront of innovation, technological advances have changed the world of microfinance. As with much of the developed world, inventions like the Internet, mobile banking, introduction of chips into credit cards, and other tools have redefined the banking industry. Although these new tools have been very beneficial to traditional banking, microfinance has found them to be lifesaving. MFIs, by nature, serve many people over a large geographic area. This means high costs for firms that wish to compete in this field. The creation and implementation of new technology helps MFIs keep costs manageable. While MFIs continue to fall behind in the adoption of innovations and IT upgrades, many leading MFIs have made technological advances "an integral part of their operational and control processes in the bid to contain costs" (Srinivasan 2010, 89). This acknowledgement is a critical step. As they continue to advance their information technology and upgrade their practices and procedures, MFIs will continue to reduce costs and deliver better services. Along with lower costs, making these changes will help them adjust to the challenges they face and increase profitability.

Banking as a whole remains very traditional in its strategy, methodology, and procedure, and microfinance is no exception. With the constant strain to reduce costs, become financially self-sustaining, and become profitable, there will be a greater push to develop. To do this, MFIs will need to find new ways to become paperless, utilize current and upcoming technological advances, and use IT services to reduce costs, make operations more efficient, and provide greater assistance to the poor who so desperately need the services. While there is much room for improvement, in recent years, MFIs have experimented and started to use more sophisticated practices.

One great example is the introduction and use of *smart cards*. Think of these as a sort of credit or debit card like the ones in your wallet. Walking around with currency can be very dangerous. One of the many differences in the financial practices of the poor and affluent individuals is that poor individuals are more likely to hold on to their money in the form of cash, which is risky and means forgoing interest it could earn. It is also awkward to carry large amounts of cash. Credit and debit cards allow individuals to spend their money without carrying large sums of cash. This additional safety and convenience is almost invaluable to the poor. Furthermore, the introduction of credit and debit cards can add numerous other benefits to the microcredit process. For example, it provides borrowers with greater flexibility in repaying and spending loans. Like any credit card, the cardholder is able to buy when shopping is convenient and products are available. Instead of taking a loan, the borrower can receive small amounts of credit for individual purchases. Additionally, the borrower might have an easier time repaying the credit. If business is doing poorly or it is a slow part of the season, the borrower can simply make a minimum payment. However, when he or she has received payment for a harvest or business is strong, that individual can pay off the whole debt. To make the process easier for the institution, the *smart cards* can automatically update interest, track past-due payments, etc. (Churchill and Frankiewicz 2006). This is a win-win for both clients and MFIs.

To make the card even more helpful, MFIs have included additional information inside the card, hence the name *smart card*. Along with all of the benefits (and downsides) of credit cards, *smart cards* also carry additional information and features that help and empower the users and the MFI. Although a standard credit card only carries personal information and currency, the *smart card* can assist the poor in many other ways:

> A smart card looks an ordinary credit or debit card, but a microchip replaces (or sometimes complements) the readable magnetic strip. Because a microchip can hold up to 800 times the information or a magnetic strip, the smart card can simultaneously manage account information, personal information (e.g., health, insurance, personal identification via biometrics), and some consumer information. (e.g., membership and loyalty clubs, buying patterns). It can also store currency and function as debit card and/or credit card (Churchill and Frankiewicz 2006, 300).

Not only can this card work as a credit or debit card, it also benefits clients by protecting their identity with security measures and by storing account and user information. Often unable to receive the same security as their high-net-worth counterparts, the poor are more vulnerable to identity theft, abuse, robbery, and the like. The features inside the *smart card* enable MFIs to protect users' identities. The chip provides a one-time number to whoever is selling the goods or services. If an identity thief tries to steal the information off the card and perform another purchase, the card will not work. Additionally, keeping track of consumer information allows MFIs to spot signs of identity or card theft. Drastic changes in spending may be a warning sign of fraud or abuse, and a credit card statement allows them to track past purchases; these also assist clients in understanding and controlling their spending.

The introduction of phones and mobile technology has had critical implications for MFIs. Cell phones have become wildly popular in developing countries, even in small rural villages. This is no surprise. Cell phones not only assist in social lives and have quality-of-life benefits, they also provide enormous advantages to businesses. Microbusinesses are able to buy and sell products over the phone, order resources, reduce communication costs and delays, increase their knowledge of the area, and so on. As in developed countries, cell phones have also led to mobile banking. The introduction of mobile banking greatly reduces wait times, operation costs, and transaction costs, and it provides business owners with greater flexibility. For example, an individual who wanted to make a loan payment or a purchase, used to have to travel to the MFI and deliver cash. However, with the addition of mobile banking, the travel is not necessary. With a few clicks, the payment can be sent and debited from the account—and a paper trail is created. The benefits of this simple change are almost innumerable. First, it is safer. A receipt for the transaction exists online, and nobody has to travel carrying large quantities of cash. Second, it saves time and reduces opportunity cost. Without the need to travel or deliver cash, the business owner can focus on making improvements or increasing sales. Third, it reduces costs. The cost of travelling is eliminated, and the transaction cost of the scenario is almost fully eliminated. Although this procedure and technology improvement is simple, its benefits are immense.

Recently, MFIs have even begun to use biometric solutions to enhance their services. This modern technology enables MFIs to use identifiers, such as fingerprints, to make secure transactions remotely. With secure systems like this in place, there is less need for staff to be present, and it substantially reduces the amount of paper records required. Surprisingly, this new method of identifying customers not only improves security, but it cuts costs for MFIs utilizing it. Furthermore, individuals who cannot read or write and do not have a signature can use their fingerprints as a secure signature. It cannot be duplicated or copied. This makes transactions easier for those with minimal educations (Goldberg and Palladini 2010, 109).

Innovations in IT services and online storage in cloud systems drastically reduces the need for paper storage, eliminating the need to rummage through old boxes. Modern IT capabilities allow MFIs to invest in cloud computing systems, which enable them to save and store documents online, work remotely, and share files between staff much more easily. Simple improvements such as this will help MFIs evolve to reach the millions around the world in need of financial services. It will help them become financially viable and able to grow. This new flexibility can free up staff to focus on more important activities like outreach, sales, and customer service. Therefore, each innovation that MFIs make can have positive implications for all parties involved.

The greatest part of innovation is that it breeds further innovation. Each additional improvement allows MFIs to save money and time that can be used to further grow and develop the process. Additionally, innovation has compounding effects in the community. For instance, one individual might benefit from receiving a cellular phone, but the benefits are compounded as the community starts to receive phones. Therefore, the introduction of modern technology into underdeveloped areas has been extremely beneficial. For example, the spread of the Internet has allowed microentrepreneurs to compare loan interest rates and providers, discover which suppliers offer the cheapest prices, learn about upcoming weather forecasts, and study best practices for their businesses. The flow of knowledge over the Internet is often missed or underappreciated. The simple communication of ideas is the lifeblood of modern entrepreneurs—and microentrepreneurs are no different. Telecommunications and the Internet have empowered the extreme poor to reach beyond their traditional regions and access a wealth of information. Increased access in these two areas will only serve to grow and improve microfinance and benefit the poor who are utilizing it.

Promotion by NGOs and the West

Microfinance has been aided by the increased awareness and promotion from the West and many international NGOs. The recognition has led to donations and investments as well as spreading the word to poor individuals who are looking for credit or financial services. For example, the announcement in 2006 that Muhammad Yunus and Grameen Bank would receive the Nobel Peace Prize for their efforts to combat poverty had a tremendous impact (Nobel Media 2014). For many MFIs, pursuing donations is a constant activity. Although this should never be the intention of any MFI, it is understandable if additional funding is required to sustain or grow operations. Publicity, such as the Nobel Prize provides MFIs with credibility and an introduction to donors and investors around the globe.

For MFIs, not all investments are made with money. Increased awareness and credibility can also bring opportunity. This can come in the form of advice, public and private assistance, better staff, strength when negotiating with regulators, discovery of new ways to innovate, and additional opportunities for growth. Therefore, bringing awareness and educating the public on the potential of microfinance is critical to the long-term survival of the industry. If governments can continue to show and grow support for MFIs and work with them, more can be accomplished. Although some governments, like the United States, have been very supportive of microfinance, not all countries share this enthusiasm. Hostility and lack of acceptance of MFIs is problematic and harmful to the poor. It is understandable for governments to scrutinize MFIs to ensure that they are beneficial. However, outright hostility threatens the ability of the poor to receive beneficial financial services. As NGOs and government agencies continue to show and grow support for MFIs, negative attitudes will change.

Additionally, NGOs and government development programs can play an important role in microfinance without ever delivering the services themselves. As MFIs struggle to grow, become financially sustainable, and reach economy of scale, NGOs and agencies can help. While leaving the risk of lending to the MFIs, NGOs can focus on providing mutually beneficial services to MFIs. Working alongside them for common goals has shown great potential. Whether it is organizing projects in tandem, splitting costs and sharing infrastructure, or coordinating outreach, these programs can advance the quality of services, reduce costs, and increase the number of services. This has the ability to save everyone time and money and increase assistance to the poor. Ideas like accepting payments for MFIs through government post offices are examples of cooperation that can be a win-win.

Microfinance's Potential

A common critique of microfinance is that it lacks substantial evidence of macro impacts. Simply said: if it so wonderful, why has it not eradicated poverty? Aside from the reasons mentioned in previous chapters, one of the most important reasons microfinance will get better is because of its potential for growth. Remenyi (2014, 54) argues:

> MFIs will always remain marginal to the big picture so long as MFIs remain small and insignificant in their outreach to poor households. Currently microfinance providers are reaching out to less than 5 percent of poor households in most poor economies. The exceptions are Bangladesh, Indonesia and Malaysia, where outreach has either approached or exceeded one-third of poor households since 1980. It is also in these three countries that the situation of the poor has improved the most over this period, and is therefore at most risk because of the Asian financial crisis of the late 1990s.

There is great potential and opportunity for microfinance to grow around the world. As it expands and develops, the organization will learn, adjust, and improve. Without delivering services on a macro scale, it is hard to accurately measure statistics and connect them to microfinance. MFIs serve millions of people around the world. However, these people tend to be rural and extremely destitute. This combination means that the process will be slow, require numerous and repeat loans to individuals, and need continuous innovation. With that said, the evidence strongly shows that MFIs deliver quality services to the poor, despite the potential of risk.

CHAPTER 10

CONCLUSION

Poverty has proven to be a persistent and unbeatable monster. It consumes the lives of billions of individuals around the world and forever limits their potential. There is nothing more cruel than the knowledge that families around the world will never be able to experience freedom, not only political liberty, but economic freedom—the chance to work and live by making choices, as opposed to being mandated. Families are trapped with the burden of debt, forced to focus only upon obtaining the next meal, rather than achieving their dreams. This struggle breeds bitterness and desperation. The grueling life of subsistence living is impossible for many in Western civilization to understand. Millions have to spend every waking moment providing for the next meal with no knowledge what the future might hold and without hope of change.

Poverty is realistically the most dangerous menace in the world. It threatens world peace, leads to war, breeds hate, helps spread diseases, and increases crime. Terrorism, ethnic and religious hatred, and conflict all arise from deep poverty. Innocent and kind people, who might never carry hate within them, become frustrated by their hopeless situation. Children grow up to see terrorism and crime as their only way out of poverty. Hate groups use the desperation of poverty as an incentive to get others to support or join them. Therefore, the implications of poverty reach well outside of the geographic confines of the extreme poor. Although Western countries may not experience poverty to the degree of developing nations, they share the burdens of poverty. Terrorism has had a monstrous impact on the United States and many other Western countries. As poverty leads to conflict, conflict to war, and war to refugees, countries in Europe are now dealing with a massive migration of refugees into their countries.

While there is no reasonable excuse for anyone to resort to violent crime or terrorism, poverty often fuels the flames of these activities. Much international terrorism comes from cities and countries that constantly struggle with poverty. Furthermore, as the United States attempts to combat drugs moving up from South and Central America, once again, poverty is part of the problem. Many of the poor in Latin America view immigration to the United States as the only solution to their troubles. Their payments to cartels to smuggle them past the border fund violence and drug trafficking in Mexico and surrounding countries. In Columbia and other Latin American countries, the poor resort to growing opium or working for cartels in order to afford the necessities of life. It is easy to argue that the poor should follow the law and avoid illegal activity, but the choice is often not that simple. Refusing to participate in the drug trade not only risks violent repercussions, but it also could mean that one's family might starve, children do not get a basic education, or families are unable to pay for simple health-care needs. Therefore, terrorists and crime organizations continue to prey upon the poor, knowing that they have no other alternatives.

These problems will not end any time soon. They will grow until the root of the problem is addressed. Poverty must be ended, and it can be. There may always be poor individuals because wealth will never be equal among the global population. Nor should it be. Rather, it is imperative that the opportunity to achieve success exist. Whether someone is trying to build a business or become a professional in the trades (engineer, scientist, doctor, lawyer, etc.) or another field, that person's success should be dependent upon hard work, dedication, and intelligence, not government approval or luck. Unfortunately, much of the poor's hope relies on handouts because Western intervention avoids alternative methods to assist.

Social Businesses

Yunus's primary principle behind microfinance was the invention of *social business*. Building upon this creation of microfinance, was the concept of businesses designed to address modern social and economic problems. Yunus (2010, 17) elaborates on this vision, stating, "The origin of the idea of social business was really quite simple: Whenever I wanted to deal with a social or economic problem, I tried to solve the problem by creating a business around it." Unlike nonprofits, businesses try to meet consumer demands with their product; social business carries the same logic. By finding a need, social businesses can enter the market and sell a product or service with the goal of using profits to expand and help more people. Social businesses do not depend upon donations or outside funding. Instead, they try to remain financially self-sustaining by providing goods and services worth purchasing. Furthermore, unlike government intervention, they enhance and expand the freedom of choice for consumers.

This philosophy and practice can be drastically expanded past microfinance and banking. Building upon the success of MFIs, social businesses have the opportunity to serve in other areas. This concept has grown in recent years and can be seen in activities all around the world. Social businesses have been created to solve various environmental challenges, pay for conservation solutions, assist poor farmers, and so on. One relevant and relatable example of a social business is coffee shops that focus on helping poor coffee growers in developing countries improve their farms. Some coffee shops have deliberately bought their coffee beans from poor farmers in developing countries. As part of their purchases, they also share best practices. Although this is a single example, this concept can evolve and take many shapes, filling an unlimited number of needs. As discussed before, there are many needs and concerns when it comes to helping the poor. This need means great potential for new social businesses.

Microfinance is not perfect. It certainly faces challenges and has yet to prove itself as a "cure-all" for poverty. With that said, it is a step in the right direction. Combined with other services, microfinance can make extreme poverty a thing of the past. As a solution, it may require a great amount of time and capital, but it is very beneficial to those that are able to access it. No one should look upon MFIs as a complete solution to poverty. That would be misleading and ineffective. However, MFIs are an important and critical factor in the fight against poverty. They provide financial solutions to the problems that many of the poor face. They invented an affordable way to help millions of rural poor pay for income-generating activity that will continue to improve their way of life. Microfinance does not force anybody to participate but rather gives options for the poor to receive credit, insurance, and other financial services that they might never have access to otherwise.

Despite any criticism that MFIs receive, the fundamental point about microfinance is that it gives the poor a choice and an opportunity to improve their situation. Like any banking activity, or for that matter any development effort, some will benefit more than others. The focus of poverty-fighting efforts should not be finding a perfect solution that helps everyone equally. Rather, development advocates should give their attention and energy to organizations and social businesses that give the poor an opportunity to improve their situation. Microfinance is a great example of this. MFIs provide financial services to the poor so that they can save, borrow, insure, and improve their situation. If MFIs offer bad customer service, explain their services poorly, or charge interest rates that are too high, then the poor have the option to not use them.

What Is the Next Step?

With all this said, microfinance is still a new industry with great potential. Its ability to grow and prosper is contingent upon the public's approach. Governments in developing countries need to welcome microfinance instead of throwing up barriers. Nonprofits must learn to work alongside MFIs as opposed to competing with them. Western governments and NGOs should work as allies in the fight against poverty and include MFIs in their plans to assist other nations. Lastly, and most importantly, people need to remain informed, engaged, and active in finding solutions to global challenges. Although it is easy to turn a blind eye to problems in other parts of the world, soon those problems will be on our doorstep. However, this does not require donations. Anyone who would like to donate can explore the Internet and find MFIs that are looking for funding to grow and reach more areas. However, it's possible to support MFIs and social businesses in other ways.

First, look for social businesses nearby: Coffee shops that work to assist farmers in developing countries, the cleaning company that is focused upon inventing cleaning solutions that are environmentally friendly, and the contractor that trains juvenile delinquents to learn trades and skills are all examples of social businesses that could be in any neighborhood. If they offer quality services and products, it's a simple step to support them. Customers should reward those who provide acceptable service and products with their patronage. It's not necessary to reduce your standards or pay substantially more. Supporting social businesses that offer needed items at reasonable prices helps these businesses grow and help additional people.

Second, consider investing in MFIs in developing countries. Many reputable MFIs are looking for investors and are willing to pay dividends or allow investors to sell the stock later for capital gains. Investors should be sure that this is the best option and should never invest more than they can afford. Furthermore, while there is always a risk of losing money with this option, it's also possible to make money while being a part of the solution to poverty. A safer option is purchasing mutual funds that include different MFIs. This possibility enables investors to incorporate helping MFIs into their retirement savings options, hire professionals that review the mutual funds for safety, gain higher returns, and provide a greater mix of organizations to assist instead of limiting their money to just one or two MFIs.

Third, some MFIs allow individuals to directly provide microloans to people in developing countries. By working as a middleman, some MFIs directly funnel donations or investments to specific microloans given to individuals. The MFI will give the investor information about the borrower, what they want to do with the loan, the borrower's story, and the eventual outcome of the microloan. This way, investors become a part of the process, feel the connection and impact of the loan, and earn a part of the interest paid on the microcredit. It is important to examine the credibility of the organization. When choosing an MFI to participate in this type of activity, look for third-party reviews and check the longevity of the program. Choose reputable organizations. Be sure to ask plenty of questions and know all the details. With that said, have fun. Do not use this process as a simple way to make profit. It is possible to lose one's money in these types of programs, and the return could be much lower than other forms of investments. Therefore, use this method as a way to save, maybe earn some money, while helping organizations that are making a difference. It is not a donation; it is an investment and participation in the process.

Final Thoughts

As microfinance continues to develop, grow, and mature, we will continue to learn more about its potential and ability to help the poor. MFIs are still learning the industry and have yet to reach hundreds of millions of potential clients. However, the evidence on the subject reflects a positive story and opportunity to make a great impact on extreme poverty. Using a combination of micro- and macroeconomic analysis on the subject, it is my conclusion that microfinance is critical in reducing poverty. While other options, such as infrastructure developments, providing basic education and health care, and decreasing government intervention and regulation must be incorporated, microfinance can make extreme poverty a part of the past. This book has examined studies of geographic areas, specific MFIs, and their clientele. The near-uniform result is a finding that MFIs are beneficial to borrowers. They provide much-needed financial services to the poor. Although they tend to charge high rates of interest, they are better other available options and are necessary for delivering services. Although critics claim that there is a death spiral of debt that borrowers accumulate, the evidence and logic do not support this argument.

More evidence is needed on the macroeconomic impact of microfinance, but this is largely irrelevant until MFIs can operate on a significant enough scale to have a macro effect. Currently, with the possible exception of Grameen Bank in Bangladesh, no MFI is large enough to have a positive or negative impact that would have national repercussions. As MFIs expand, more research can be done on the subject. The research that has measured the outcomes of participants generally reflects positive outcomes with higher incomes, greater assets, and better living conditions after borrowers receive microcredit. Furthermore, MFIs continue to grow, develop, and evolve to adjust to customer needs. With technological upgrades, the creation of procedures, and discovery of better business practices, MFIs have improved their services to meet the needs of a challenging population group. MFIs have already shown themselves to be a major contributor in combating deep poverty. As they continue to evolve and improve, MFIs will be able to deliver better results and make greater strides in reducing poverty, creating a world with more possibilities.

BIBLIOGRAPHY

Alila, Patrick O., and Poul O. Pedersen. *Negotiating Social Space: East AfricanMicroenterprises*. Trenton, NJ: Africa World Press, 2001.

Armendariz, Beatriz, and Jonathan Morduch. *The Economics of Microfinance*. 2d. ed.Cambridge, Mass: MIT Press, 2010.

Arun, T., D. Hulme, and S. Rutherford. "Finance for the Poor: The Way Forward?" In*Microfinance: a Reader*. Edited by David Hulme and Thankom Arun, 7-16. London:Routledge, 2009.

Bowen, M. K. "Risk as a Constraint to Microenterprise Growth." *Negotiating Social Space:East African Microenterprises*, edited by Patrick O. Alila and Poul O. Pedersen, 291-304.Trenton, NJ: Africa World Press, 2001.

Brainard, Lael. "Compassionate Conservatism Confronts Global Poverty." *The WashingtonQuarterly* 26, no. 2 (2003): 149-69. Accessed February 16, 2016. <https://www.brookings.edu/wp-content/uploads/2016/06/20030301.pdf>.

Christen, Robert Peck, and Deborah Drake. "The New Reality of Microfinance." In *TheCommercialization of Microfinance: Balancing Business and Development*. Edited byDeborah Drake and Elisabeth Rhyne, 2-21. Bloomfield, Connecticut: Kumarian Press, 2002.

Churchill, Craig, and Cheryl Frankiewicz. *Making Microfinance Work: Managing for Improved Performance.* Geneva: International Labor Office, 2006.

Churchill, Craig Farren. *Protecting the Poor: a Microinsurance Compendium.* Geneva,Switzerland: International Labor Office, 2006.

Copestake, James G., Alyson Brody, Martin Greeley, and Katie Wright-Revolledo. *Money with amission.* London: ITDG, 2005.

Daphnis, Franck, and Bruce Ferguson. *Housing Microfinance: a Guide to Practice.* Bloomfield,Connecticut: Kumarian Press, 2004.

Deubel, Tara. "Banking on Culture: Microcredit as Incentive for Cultural Conservation in Mali.In *Microfinance: Perils and Prospects.* Edited by Jude Fernando. London: Routledge,2006.

Ebimobowei, Appah, John M. Sophia, and Soreh Wisdom. "An Analysis of Microfinance andPoverty Reduction in Bayelsa State of Nigeria." Kuwait Chapter of *Arabian Journal of Business and Management Review* 1, no. 7 (2012): 38-57.

Goldberg, Mike, and Eric Palladini. *Managing Risk and Creating Value with Microfinance.*Washington, DC: World Bank, 2010.

Hemlin, M., O. Sjöberg, and P. Ronnås. *Institutional Adjustment For Economic Growth: SmallScale Industries and Economic Transition in Asia and Africa.* Aldershot, England:Ashgate, 1998.

Islam, Tazul. *Microcredit and Poverty Alleviation.* Aldershot, Hants, England: Ashgate, 2007.

Kloppenburg, Norbert. "Microfinance Investment Funds: Where Wealth Creation Meets PovertyReduction." In *Microfinance Investment Funds: Leveraging Private Capital forEconomic Growth and Poverty Reduction.* Edited by Ingrid Matthäus-Maier and J. D.Von Pischke, 1-7. Berlin: Springer, 2006.

Ledgerwood, Joanna. *Microfinance Handbook: An Institutional and Financial Perspective.*Washington, DC: World Bank, 1999.

Mannan, M. A. *Growth and development of small enterprise: the case of Bangladesh.* Aldershot:Avebury, 1993.

Matthäus-Maier Ingrid, and J. D. Von Pischke. *New Partnerships for Innovation inMicrofinance.* Berlin: Springer, 2008.

Pagura, Maria E. *Expanding the Frontier in Rural Finance: Financial Linkages and StrategicAlliances.* Rugby, Warwickshire, UK: Practical Action Pub., 2008.

Pedersen, Poul O. "East African Microenterprises Negotiating Social Space: An Introduction." In*Negotiating Social Space: East African Microenterprises,* edited by Patrick O. Alila andPoul O. Pedersen, 1-24. Trenton, NJ: Africa World Press, 2001.

Prize for 2006 to Muhammad Yunus and Grameen Bank—Press Release. Nobel Media AB.2014. Accessed September 18, 2015.

Remenyi, Joe. "Is there a 'State of the Art' in Microfinance." In *Microfinance and Povertyalleviation : Case Studies from Asia and the Pacific.* Edited by J. Remenyi and B.Quiñones, 25-64. New York: Routledge, 2014.

Roodman, David Malin. *Due Diligence: An Impertinent Inquiry into Microfinance.* Washington,DC: Center For Global Development, 2012.

Rutherford, Stuart. "The Need To Save." In *Microfinance: a Reader.* Edited by David Hulmeand Thankom Arun, 36-44. London: Routledge, 2009.

Sharma, Manohar, and Gertrud Buchenrieder. "Impact of Microfinance on Food Security andPoverty Alleviation: A Review and Synthesis of Empirical Evidence." In *The Triangle ofMicrofinance: Financial Sustainability, Outreach, and Impact.* Edited by Manfred Zellerand Richard L. Meyer, 221-240. Baltimore: Johns Hopkins University Press, 2002.

Shikwati, James. "SPIEGEL Interview with African Economics Expert: "For God's Sake, PleaseStop the Aid!"" Interview by Thilo Thielke. Translation by Patrick Kessler. Aus DemSpiegel. July 4, 2005. Accessed August 30, 2016.

Srinivasan, N. *Microfinance India: State of the Sector Report 2010.* Thousand Oaks, California:Sage, 2010.

Webster, Leila, and Peter Fidler. *The Informal Sector and Microfinance Institutions In WestAfrica.* Washington, DC: World Bank, 1996.

White, Victoria, and Campion, Anita. "Journey from NGO to Regulated MFI." In *TheCommercialization of Microfinance: Balancing Business and Development.* Edited byDeborah Drake and Elisabeth Rhyne, 2-21. Bloomfield, Connecticut: Kumarian Press,2002.

Yunus, Muhammad, and Alan Jolis. *Banker to the Poor: Micro-lending and the Battle AgainstWorld Poverty.* New York, NY: Public Affairs, 2003.

Yunus, Muhammad, and Karl Weber. *Building social business: The new kind of capitalism thatserves humanity's most pressing needs.* New York: Public Affairs, 2010.

Yunus, Muhammad, and Karl Weber. *Creating a World Without Poverty: Social Business andthe Future of Capitalism.* New York: Public Affairs, 2007.

ABOUT THE AUTHOR

Samuel Wahlen believes that free market solutions can solve world poverty. He has been quoted in numerous news stories on economic and political issues and works as a banker in Racine, Wisconsin. He serves as President of the Racine Taxpayers Association, previously Chairman of the Racine County Republican Party, is on the Board of Commissioners and Chair of the Finance Committee for the Housing Authority of Racine County, and has been involved in numerous philanthropic activities.

Printed in the United States
By Bookmasters